T0095460

Life Lived in God's Hands

LIFE LIVED IN GOD'S HANDS

One Man's Journey Back Home

BILL BRACK

iUniverse, Inc.
Bloomington

Life Lived in God's Hands
One Man's Journey Back Home

iUniverse books may be ordered through booksellers or by contacting:

iUniverse
1663 Liberty Drive
Bloomington, IN 47403
www.iuniverse.com
1-800-Authors (1-800-288-4677)

ISBN: 978-1-4697-3698-3 (sc)
ISBN: 978-1-4697-3700-3 (hc)
ISBN: 978-1-4697-3699-0 (ebk)

Printed in the United States of America

iUniverse rev. date: 02/10/2012

CONTENTS

Dedication

"I thank God, whom I serve with a clear conscience the way my forefathers did . . . For I am mindful of the sincere faith within you, which first dwelt in your grandmother Lois and your mother Eunice, and I am sure that it is in you as well . . . Therefore do not be ashamed of the testimony of our Lord or of me his prisoner . . ." 2 Timothy 1:3-8a

Today I embark on a task that I have intended to begin many times for many months. Perhaps this undertaking is a rite of passage that many have pursued before me as they began to grapple with their own mortality. But for me this is not merely spurred by the awareness that I am mortal. At this writing my health is good and my strength as it has been, so the reflections here are not penned under urgency. For me, this is a sort of commissioning I feel deep in my spirit, a calling if you will. The purpose I here intend is that my children specifically, and by extension, my grandchildren, and through them, my posterity know the life of faith that has been my journey.

A very small part of my journey has been in full time Christian work. It has occurred to me that while that portion of my journey was significant and important, it comprises the majority of what my children know of the totality of my journey. The truth is that the spiritual fires of my life began early and with experiences so rich they formed, transformed, and made me who I am. These fires motivated my vocational choices, education, and moves along the way. It is these fires that I want to communicate and give chronology so that my children will know and better understand "the rock from whence I was hewn," and from whence they too have come.

I'm under no illusion here. I understand that this writing will take time and sometimes be painful as I seek to honestly present not only the victories and highpoints of a life lived in God's hands but also the failures and difficulties that have accompanied it. But I also know even at this beginning point that I feel His presence, direction and pleasure again and again as I write.

I have three wishes for this writing. First, I hope you will more clearly understand the greatness of God's love for you and that He demonstrates it at every turn of our lives. Second, I hope you will better appreciate your divine heritage and the manifold blessings that have been deposited to your spiritual account. Last, I hope my journey will inspire you to settle upon His great path and follow His perfect lead wherever it may take you.

Finally, as you know, I'm not a writer in the true sense of the term. I labor with each word, sentence, and paragraph to make each correct, editing and re-editing to make it the best I can. But this labor of love is born in the Father's heart and is here lain before you from both of your fathers, one heavenly, the other painfully clay. I hope as you read these lines you will sense the spirit of us both. Daddy

Prologue

We were young, kids really, doing what kids do: playing games, oblivious of the future, trying to make sense of our little world, hoping to not be too conspicuous or different from everybody else. There was nothing special about us, nothing that made us better or worse than anybody else. Care free, we were totally unaware that He was weaving His presence in our lives. Not all of us, of course, but some.

Our hopes for the future were at best vague. We were young, and the future was as close as our next breath yet as far away as the stars. We knew neither mortality nor reasoning. We simply lived moment to moment, swinging on swings, staring at clouds that looked like zebras, unaware that He was weaving His presence in our lives. Not all of us, of course, but some.

Time passed: we set aside childish games. The world became more complicated and more serious. We established relationships, pursued dreams, grew up, sort of. We went separate ways and played new, "grown up" games. We looked for gold or self esteem or the perfect this or that. We tucked our insecurities where others couldn't see them and went about the business and busyness of our lives, all the while unaware that He was weaving His presence in our lives. Not all of us, of course, but some.

He let us roam for a while. He let us try our wings, buy that gadget, make impressions. He allowed us time to succeed or fail, to run whatever race we were running. He took the backseat and let us drive down bumpy roads, tires screeching, going fast around curves that led nowhere. He seemed neither surprised by nor disappointed in our many wrong turns as He was weaving His presence into our lives.

Some of us at some point arrived at the disillusionment of the chase. We either had what we wanted or realized we never would or didn't want what we had five minutes after we got it. Some of us arrived at dead ends and others arrived at the pot of gold at the end of the rainbow only to find out that it too was a dead end. We discovered that we were mortal, flawed, and broken. Not all of us, of course, but some, and all the while He was weaving His presence in our lives.

Sure, looking back now we can see His doing. We can see when He carried us or when He rescued us from our many miscues and mistakes; how He helped us navigate the throes of our lives, bear its pains, make sense of things; how He enabled us to succeed or fail, whichever it took so we could come to the end of ourselves and realize He was there all the while, weaving His presence in our lives. Not all of us, of course, but some.

Gradually, the games gave way to reality. We finally put away childishness and no longer played hide and seek or "whoever dies with the most toys wins." We surrendered to the fact that we were for the most part empty. We had filled our lives with the "its" of life and they had left us pretty much unsatisfied. And in our despair or sanctified good sense we turned to the One who had been patiently weaving His presence in our lives. Not all of us, of course, but some.

And those of us who did, found a life better than our dreams, greater than our failures, and higher than our goals. We wished we had turned our silly hearts and strangely empty lives over to Him earlier than we did. But we have learned and now know that the wayward course of our lives serves His purpose, too. We have found that He leaves no stone unturned, wastes no wrong decision, and loses no opportunity. Rather, with glorious relentlessness, He pursues us still, weaving His unmistakable presence in our lives. Yes! All of us, not just some.

CHAPTER 1

Before the Beginning

It happens quite frequently, mostly at busy intersections or Interstate off-ramps. I've often wondered what happened, what caused it? How does one become a beggar and dependent on hand outs? I see them stand there, sign in hand, and wonder what life experiences or traumas have led to this: homeless, hungry, alone.

I try to imagine them as children: happy, playful, a bright future with all the promise of any one of us. Did childhood dreams take him to exotic places where he would conquer kingdoms and slay dragons? Did she play with Barbie dolls and serve make believe tea and have all night slumber parties? Did he dream of being a football hero or she hope to be crowned the homecoming queen? In the age of innocence, was all good and free and their only limits the greatness of childhood imaginations?

What choices along the way set in motion a journey that has brought him here? Was it just a string of bad luck? Was it drugs or alcohol? Was it the unspeakable horrors of war? Was it the unbearable sorrow of love lost? Was he weak of moral fiber and strength, so that the weight of the world caused his crash? Was he merely the weaker one in this survival-of-the-fittest world? What was it that brought that young child with so much hope to the place he is now, standing in the street all alone, asking strangers for bread? And, WHY IS HE NOT ME?

Over the years of my life I have grappled with this, not constantly or relentlessly, but steadily. To my great shame, many times I have been heartless and skeptical, drawing conclusions from the unsubstantiated "facts" as I saw them. But I've met some of the homeless and talked openly with them, and they with me. In short, I've come to some resolutions about this. One is that the answer to most of my questions is "yes". Many homeless people have suffered devastating losses that have so ripped their souls; they simply were unable to recover. They turned for comfort where they could find it: some to drugs, some, aloneness. In the affluence that is America, there is no limit to the ways to medicate one's pain or hide one's fears. Many rejected their loved ones, while others were rejected by them, as they sought to cope or make sense of their lives. There are always, of course, two sides to every story and, in the final analysis, there is only One who knows the whole story.

It is this "One" who helps explain my deeper questions; Why not me? Why am I not that beggar—without family, shelter or food? Why am I not the one with a sign in my hand and a pack on my back? What did I do right that he did wrong? And, why is he not me?

The Maestro of the Cloud

When I try to understand the depths of the Father's love and plan for me, it quickly becomes overwhelming: His fantastic attention to detail, His steadfastness amidst a clamoring free will, His opus performed flawlessly through the years both present and past. It is only because of Him and His power to give sneak-peeks, both forward and back, that I can catch the smallest glimpse of what He has done to make me who I am. Mine is not a solitary walk of faith; I am no self-made man, but one seated on the high shoulders of those who have gone before.

Here is the real tragedy: My knowledge about these giants who forged my faith before my birth is so very sketchy. I admit this here to my shame that these grand folks have died without my desire being pricked, as it is now, to know them and the depths of a God that forged the great spiritual canyon in which I now stand. That is not to say that all have been spiritual or even interested in God, but it is to say that God has so orchestrated the music that it bears the certain sound of His purpose in me.

Some were Baptists, some were Methodists, and some were Missionary Alliance. Some carried a deeper walk of faith than I can even imagine, while others strolled along the edges, not truly committed at all. But the consistent chord that came to be was one of an unmistakable faith.

My grandfather and mother on my mom's side were probably Baptists and Methodists. I have no real evidence that my grandfather Royal was a spiritual man. Indeed, I'm not sure he even gave "religion" the time of day. But he married a girl of deep Methodist roots and there is sufficient evidence that she was a woman of faith from a family of faith. Her spiritual life was nurtured through the old circuit rider preachers of the late nineteenth and early twentieth century in rural Georgia. Her family was well known to me since it was to this family we'd vacation and spend easy summer days. Uncle John Wesley Carrington, my mom's uncle, was a grand fellow with a quick wit and an easy way. He'd often sling his leg over a rocking chair on the porch and tell of his life and times. We'd attend the Methodist church where he was a leader.

Though we know very little about my dad's family, his mother had a sister who I knew as Aunt Ruby. She was a devout Christian nurse who served in New Jersey with the Missionary Alliance church, and there seems to be evidence that she may have even served as a missionary of sorts. I knew this aunt from our many trips to St. Petersburg, Florida, where we would visit and go to church with her during my growing up years. While little is concretely known, it isn't a far stretch to believe that this root was also in her sister, my grandmother Brack.

Beyond these few references, I know little and have many questions. Premiere among them are these: How far back did the work of God go before me? When did it start? I feel sure that Heaven will chime the answers that time has lost and I am satisfied that the God who came to me did so on the prayers and faithfulness of my ancestors past. But even if God only started with my mother and father, His presence so filled my life through them it is unquestioned.

My mother moved to Florida when she was eight years old. She went to church her entire life, attending the old Second Baptist Church of Ocala, because it was close enough to walk to from her home. Through those years she was a member of the Young Women's Auxiliary, a mission's organization. A friend introduced her to Barney Brack and the grand story of this courtship was that my mother made my father promise to go to church with her on Sunday before she would agree to go "out" with him. Later she would volunteer in the nursery, keep Sunday school records, and open her home to cottage prayer meetings for revival and fellowships for the youth.

My father had a difficult youth. His parents divorced when he was quite young. There is some evidence that his father, my grandfather, was an alcoholic and a hard man. At any rate, both of my dad's parents passed away while he was in his teens. Good people came into his life and helped him survive, but my mom is credited with turning his heart toward God. Sometime after they were married, Daddy accepted Christ as his savior. From that time forward, he was an active member in the Baptist church I grew up in, first teaching a boys' Sunday school class and eventually the senior men, and serving as a deacon for as long as I can remember.

My clearest memories of my dad studying his Bible with his Sunday school quarterly in hand, preparing to teach his men's class. I remember seeing his hand-writings in the margins and the underlined verses that spoke to his life. Oh, how I would love to have that pot of gold now. I recall his habit of writing his tithe check every Sunday morning, sitting at the dining room table. I can still see him praying at the table over our meals, his hands joined to Mama's and ours. I remember riding to church between Mama and Daddy in the front seat (I think this probably speaks more to his efforts to keep me from misbehaving than to my status as favorite son) and how much I loved being there. I remember how effortless his walk of faith seemed to me.

Together, Mama and Daddy were an unbeatable team. They loved each other with every breath. I cannot remember a single harsh word spoken between them in my entire life. They simply went about living the joys and hardships of life, breathing in and out, and in the process showing me how life was supposed to be: you love the Lord, take care of your family, keep your commitments, and live in quiet peace. These simple truths were planted in me long before I even knew it, long before I myself would need them with a family of my own.

What a rude awakening to leave that cocoon and discover others were abused by their parents, sometimes beaten or otherwise assaulted. How amazed I was to find out that other children's parents fussed and fought constantly and spoke harshly and with malice of intent. I was shocked when I found out that others did not experience a family unit that crafted a moral code of absolute truth and faith. What a blow it was to find that other children had parents who were two-faced, pretending to be one thing in public, but being something horribly different in private, and blow of blows, some of these children attended church with me. How surprised I was to learn that there are others with no church connection whatsoever, some with no consciousness of God at all.

But for me, I knew I was loved by a mother and a father who demonstrated it every moment of every day. I never wondered if my daddy was coming home after work, or if he would he be sober, or if he would be angry. He always came home, right on time. It never crossed my mind that Mama would not have supper on the stove, hugs at the ready, and Daddy on her mind. I have come to cherish the memory of her daily admonition, "Get ready for supper, Daddy will be home any minute," and he always was. And when he walked in the door, he took his hat off and gave Mama a kiss before anything else happened. I feel pain for those who may read this and have no idea what I'm talking about.

Simply put, my mama and daddy were giants. Theirs was a faith that lived. It brought laughter and joy, steadiness and peace, and it brought reality. Their faith was true and without guile. It wasn't put on for church and then taken off when they got home. It was real and it was on open display at my house every day of my youth.

Amazing Grace

So, why is he not me? Why am I not the one at the intersection of Despair and Loneliness? What did he do wrong that I did right? Nothing! Absolutely nothing! Maybe God the Father knew I would be irretrievably lost in my weak state had he not sheltered me thus. Maybe He knew I couldn't survive in a harsh environment. Maybe He understood how fragile my faith would be, how weak my resolve in the face of even minor adversity. Maybe He understood my greatest weaknesses, and so, He wrapped and nurtured me in the arms of His love. Maybe without this cast of "witnesses," right here, right this very instant, I would be there myself: homeless, hungry, alone.

But for whatever reasons, this I know. The faith that was once my mama's and daddy's is now mine. How could it not be? I am the passive beneficiary of a spiritual heritage that is mine simply because of the amazing grace of a sovereign God who chose to place me where I could not lose.

As I write now, I see it clearer still. My parents were Christians. And that same love that would not let them go, wouldn't let me go either. That faith that served them through their lives has served me through mine. And the Father who shepherded them through death's door will surely shepherd me.

I join with the writer of the New Testament book of Hebrews to declare that I too am surrounded by a great cloud of witnesses. Not just Abraham of old or names made famous by biblical exploits, but by those I've known in flesh and blood, those whose lives demonstrated their faith in plain view. They lean over a banister and cheer me on now, beckoning me to pursue the greatest prize. They stretch out their hands and lift me up when I fall and applaud when I rise. They remind me now, more than ever, that I was hewn from a Rock greater than me, greater than them. And they let me know that the Father has loved me from before I was born, and if the Bible is to be believed, His love has been my portion since before the beginning.

CHAPTER 2

How Firm a Foundation

Though the spiritual fires were carefully set even before I was born, the early years of my life were filled with multiple layers of rich encounters of the life-forming and transforming kind. I started "church proper" at three weeks old and never stopped through my teen years. From being rocked by Mrs. Harward in the nursery to youth choir as a senior high school student, precious servants of the Redeemer's great love surrounded me, nurturing and pointing me steadily onward. Being raised in a strong, conservative Baptist church provided me with a foundation of conscience and faith for which I am eternally grateful.

. . . Raised to walk in newness of life . . .

I was active in every aspect of Wyomina Park Baptist Church. Sunday school teachers, pastors, youth leaders, and lifelong friends filled my world. Sunday was a day looked forward to, and I can't remember a time I ever wanted to go anywhere else more than to church. I wanted to dress and wear my hair just like Brother Houser, sing like Ted Hays, preach like Brother Cooper Marshall, be a deacon like my dad, and live like a Christian. Vacation Bible Schools, Royal Ambassadors, Sunday school attendance, scripture memorization, Training Union, Youth Choir practices, socials, Marion Baptist Associational Youth Rallies, Bible Sword Drills, and a myriad of other church related activities: these were the building blocks of my childhood, youth, and faith.

My mother tells the foreshadowing story of my bent toward a pastoral future. I would come home from Sunday services, go to my room, stand in front of the full length mirror, don my coat and tie, King James Bible in hand, and "preach." I remember doing exactly that: pretending I was the preacher, "preaching" a passionate sermon, calling sinners to open their hearts' doors to Jesus and come for salvation, inviting sinners to "come home." I would beckon as I had so often heard and mimic almost every preacher's plea. "We're going to sing one more stanza and as we do, you come." I'd sing the verses of *Just As I Am,* a song that was a staple, whose verses I had memorized early on from the *Broadman Hymnal,* from which we sang every Sunday. I would shake the hand of responders, and introduce them to the congregation who would then receive them into "the full fellowship" of the church because of their "statement of faith." A child's play, yes, but certainly evidence of God's deep call and hold in my life early on.

When I was eight years old, our church was "having a revival." Sometimes "revival" means a schedule of meetings that go for about a week or two. This revival turned into a real move of God. It was at this revival that I first became convinced of my own sin and the consequences of it. I "walked the aisle" one night, a ritual practiced regularly in our tradition. I shook the preacher's hand, prayed a sinner's prayer, and asked Christ to be my Lord and Savior. Before the week was out, I was baptized by immersion in the church baptismal tank. I remember the experience as both frightening and solemn. I was "raised to walk in newness of life."

One might rightfully be skeptical about an eight-year-old boy's conversion or even his true awareness of his sin. I don't really have a theological argument for or against such a thing, but one thing has convinced me of the reality and the authenticity of that experience. For as long as I can remember, I have always had a God consciousness, that is, an awareness of His presence and a tender knowing He was in my life. I can't fully explain it and I certainly can't quantify it, but I know it to be true. My spirit was pricked and made alive, and there has been no time since that I have entirely lost that consciousness. Many times I have stumbled, failed, fallen, or otherwise defected, but even in those times, He has never let me go. As my life matured, my understanding enlightened and my heart changed. I believe it all started at that humble revival so long ago.

... Transforming Growth ... The Teenage Years

It was the best of times! I enjoyed most of the years of my youth, though there were times I felt inferior in many ways. My school grades never approached the level they would later on in college and seminary. In fairness to myself and the teachers who labored with me, I didn't really try to be a good student. I admit that I was comfortable with academic mediocrity. I had no interest in school and only wanted to get out. The path of least resistance was my theme, and it plagued me even as my spiritual life took off.

My teen years were filled with significant names. Francis Allegood was my most memorable Sunday school teacher. He was assigned the Junior Boys class, and in that class I met friends who helped me become a better Christian. I mention their names here not because they were flawless. The truth is, none of us understood the depths we were being called to at the time, but Allen Harrell, Mac Harrell, Richard Hale, and Jimmy Dan Walton became my constant companions throughout those years. Mr. Allegood took us water skiing and we had class parties at his house. I thought he was the coolest "old person" I knew. He had a ready laugh and a balance that made me always want to be at church.

As time passed, a youth choir was assembled, and I fancied myself a singer. Ted Hays, our music director and youth pastor (though we just called him Ted) and our choir quickly became the focal point of my life. Our church celebrated the youth, and our numbers grew throughout my high school years. Parents opened their homes (as they had done for the youth well before I came along), and we'd have fellowships and food—that cost us nothing. Many were the times we'd gather around a family's piano and sing the songs we loved at the top of our lungs. I'm sure we had cliques and personality quirks that are unavoidable for adolescents from time to time, but I don't remember such. We all seemed to get along well and enjoy each other's company. For me, there was no better place to ever be than at choir practice and hanging around my friends at church. I even attempted some evangelism and invited a friend or two from school into this unique group. At one point I even ventured a voice lesson with Ted.

Reverend Cooper Marshall came to our Baptist church in my eighth grade year. I loved him from the moment I met him. (It probably didn't hurt that he had a daughter my age for whom I fell right away, though I'm pretty sure she never felt the same. Cindy and her sister Debbie were the coolest of them all.) His leadership of our church made my teen years far more than just having fun. His life and ministry produced a spiritual hunger and energy in me. God was proactive in my life, setting a course for faith in me that was foundational, and it has never stopped growing since.

Sunday nights, the youth choir would sing, clad in silver robes. This was in the late 1960s and early 1970s. Our culture was changing rapidly, and the music we sang reflected a style more contemporary than traditional. I think this "progressive" music kept us all in church to some extent. After we sang a special each Sunday night, we'd go down from the choir loft and take our places on the first three or four pews on the right side of the sanctuary. Wyomina Park Baptist Church knew how to embrace us and make us feel good and important.

As Brother Marshall preached Sunday after Sunday, I felt that God Himself spoke to me. Sunday nights were the time I felt His presence more than any other. I recall being under a consistent cloud of conviction as he preached. Often, more times than I care to admit, I'd step from the pew where Jimmy Dan, Allen Harrell and I sat, and walk forward to "rededicate" my life to Christ. Surely Brother Marshall must have gotten a little agitated at my youth, but he never showed anything but true love and understanding. He prayed with me each time, and was a most amazing and constant encouragement to me.

Now I say I was under conviction and there was a good reason for this. By the time I was an early teenager, I had found it hard to be a "Christian" in front of my peers. I had a lengthy battle with such sins as pornography, cursing, sneaking tobacco, and in general living a double life. And it was this inconsistency that caused such spiritual conflict in me for many years, stretching into my young adult life. I'll share more on this later, but mention it here in brief because it plagued me throughout the years of my youth. When we sang "Amazing Grace, how sweet the sound, that saved a wretch like me," I was that wretch and I felt it to my very bones. The conflict often sabotaged my quest to be fully "Christian", and Sunday night conviction and repentance became the norm. But for me, my many "rededications" were about more than just a young boy's wrestling match with the devil. It was also a knowing that His hand was on my life. I had a deep knowing that in spite of my hypocrisy and inconsistency, He wanted me in special ways that many of my friends didn't seem to share. While we all seemed genuinely committed to living for Him (and several from our youth group surrendered to "full-time Christian service"), I felt a special sense of his drawing me personally, and even though my failures were always the elephant in the room of my spiritual life, the divine presence was always there, calling me deeper, and the longing for His life in me was profoundly real.

Please understand, I was a real teenager with the same mindsets, perceptions, and hormones that teenagers through the years have endured. I thought my parents were out of touch and old fashioned, that our music was better than theirs, and that they were, of course, too strict. My brushes with temptation and subsequent failures with them only made these adolescent perceptions more acute and my struggle to be the Christian I knew I was supposed to be more difficult. But despite my own struggles with evil and my many failures, I need you to know that I had many close encounters with the Living God during my youth. It became obvious to me that His was a love "that would not let me go," so faithful was this Father-God who was jealous for His son.

Of these many encounters, I will point out two in particular here. ***The first occurred*** Labor Day weekend of my ninth grade year. Our family went to Lake Waldena, to swim and have lunch. This local lake was big enough for boating and small enough to swim around. I'm not sure when we first discovered this place, but by the time of this event it had become a family favorite. We loved to canoe around it also, often disembarking to climb a tree and jump into the water from what seemed a great height. We'd leisurely swim for hours on end. Many times we'd just head out swimming around the lake unsupervised, and that's what we were doing on this particular day.

This story has been told many times and has achieved the status of family lore; of how as we swam, a boat from the other side of the lake headed our way, of how it followed a direct path to where we were swimming. I think we all saw it coming but we couldn't avoid it. As I remember it, while my brother Gene froze in place and sort of watched it coming, my good friend Allen, Joan (now my brother Gene's wife) and me dove to the bottom in a vain attempt at avoiding disaster. I was hit by the boat, and later learned that I'd been cut deep into my back, through three layers of muscle, and that the rudder had come within a hair of puncturing my lung, and if that had happened, I would have drowned before they could have gotten me out of the water. I was rushed to the hospital where I underwent major surgery (over one hundred stitches), but made a full recovery.

Unaware of the seriousness of my injuries, I was quickly carted to Ocala's Monroe Memorial Hospital, lying in the back of a stranger's car, and I was scared. I wondered how bad I was hurt and remember asking the drivers, "Will I be okay?" Their answer was meant to reassure me. "Sure you will!" But the big puddle of blood that surrounded me was enough to question their surety and I thought of death. While maybe not probable, I thought that death was at least a possibility. I began to seriously think about God's calling and drawing me to Himself. I wondered if He really might have a divine purpose for me that I had not fully realized or embraced.

After surgery and release from the hospital, I continued to think about the event that could have ended my life, and these thoughts pressed me to give serious attention to God's hand on me. I had no "death bed conversion," but I did feel a sense of urgency to seek out and discover His calling and purpose in my life. Over the next several days, I found my thoughts centered on a feeling that He might be calling me generally into "full-time Christian service" of some kind, whatever that meant (and I was deeply concerned that that might mean being a missionary to Africa, wherever that was), but more specifically, I felt that He was "calling me to preach," a common term we used for someone in full-time Christian service, like a pastor.

By the first Sunday after the boating accident, I had made a decision of sorts. I came to church ready to publicly declare my "call to preach" to our congregation. As the invitational hymn was played, I stepped from my pew and walked to the front where Brother Marshall stood waiting for those who wanted to "get saved" or "join the church" or "rededicate their lives" to the Lord. I shook his hand and whispered that I believed that God was calling me to preach. I vaguely remember him conveying my intentions to the congregations that day but that he wanted to follow up with me personally later, an event I remember really looking forward to.

I'm not sure how soon the meeting took place (Brother Marshall was a prompt man who to my knowledge always honored his word and commitments, so I'm sure it was soon after my Sunday declaration and without delay on his part), but I do remember the essence of his instruction: I was a young person, a ninth grader. I should stay in school and get good grades. I then should go to college, maybe the University of Florida or some Baptist college and get a B.A., majoring perhaps in Business or Finance. After graduation, I should attend a Baptist seminary, a three year course of study where I would learn theology, Hebrew and Greek, Christian education, and philosophy. After graduation from seminary, I would be ordained to preach by the first church that "called" me to be their pastor in the Baptist traditional way. I remember we had prayer, but that prayer is a blur to me now (actually, that prayer was a blur to me then too), but I'm sure Brother Marshall was gracious and loving, and placed me and my future in God's hands.

I don't know what I expected. I don't know what I thought it might mean or what requirements must be met to "preach," but I remember that meeting as cold water poured on the fire of my soul, and my head reeled as I tried to wrap my mind around what it all meant. Good grades? High School graduation? College? Seminary? Eleven years? My grades in ninth grade were not failing but they were not exactly worthy of a person bound for seven years of higher education. And I hated school! How much was such an education going to cost anyway? Who pays for that? How would I, how could I pay for that?

But my real dilemma was more than the money for college and seminary, much more. The price I had to pay was the price of following a calling I believed came from God while clinging to the wayward heart of a teenager who wasn't very good at being what he really wanted to be. This dichotomy produced an inner conflict that wouldn't be resolved for years, many, many years. And through those years I kept trying to define a calling I knew I had but didn't have much of a handle on.

The second encounter came a few years later when I was in high school. Unlike the first, this encounter was not precipitated by accident or fear. Our church was having revival meetings with Dr. Paul Meigs, an elderly statesman of the Florida Baptist Convention. During this "scheduled" revival, "real" revival broke out in a powerful way, and its strongest waves flowed through the youth. For three weeks, we stayed in the sanctuary after the meetings ended, praying and crying out, hungering for more of God. Adults took turns monitoring the youth, making sure that nothing "unbiblical" took place and that no one went off the deep end (at least that's what I thought they were there for).

That revival so touched our hearts that many in our youth group made professions of faith and several expressed the desire to go into ministry. As for me, I remember praying and crying, wanting the fullness of God in my life like never before. This was a real change in me that helped move me forward in my spiritual life and journey. It wasn't about what God might want from my life or what He wanted me to do as much as it was an understanding that was beginning to come to me: God wanted me, like the old adage that says, "I don't want what you have, I want you."

This was no small shift in my thinking. It was seismic. For the first time I began to grapple with the idea that a real friendship relationship with God might be possible, and that that relationship was to be more than me giving up my dreams and life for Him. A seed was sown, a seed ever so small—that God wanted me. He wanted a relationship with me.

Before this time, I was pretty sure that God was mostly an angry presence. He saw me, alright, and He didn't much like what He saw. I had lived under a cloud of condemnation for quite some time and to be honest it was what I deserved. But it was also what I had come to expect. The thought process went something like this: "God loves me, but He will not tolerate MY sin. He hates sin, and His holiness cannot abide MY sin. MY sin, no matter how small it may seem to me, separates me from Him and His love. Therefore, if I want His acceptance and love, I must rid myself of MY sin."

There is truth here. The Bible does speak to this: sin does in fact separate us from Him, and I was thoroughly versed in this "demand side" thinking. But this new, tiny seed gave me a glimmer of hope. I didn't understand it then, and I'm pretty sure I don't understand it fully now, but I somehow became aware that what God wants is a loving relationship with people. I say "aware" because it has taken almost all of my life to come to a place to really believe His love is so great that it allows Him to accept me as I am; weaknesses, failures, mistakes, struggles and all. The problem, however, is this: How does one rid oneself of sin? I have wrestled to come to some personal understanding of this seemly simple question, but my revelations have come slowly and my understanding slower still. But here is where I have landed: God has a three pronged approach as he deals with people. First, motivated by a cataclysmic, earth-shattering love that no man can comprehend, God must do something so that he can love man despite of man's sin. If He cannot come to us in our sin, if He cannot look upon us because of our sin, we are hopelessly doomed, for we are unable to cleanse ourselves from our sin. We can conquer neither our sin nature nor our lesser sin habits by sheer will. He must make the first move. This He did in Christ, in time before time. Christ, slain from the foundations of the world. Second, like a troubadour wooing his lover, God woos us with His firm, gentle love. His love comes to us with infinite variety, but it comes to us all. None is beyond His reach. None can say that He has not loved them. His love melts the coldest heart. His love goes out through the universes and to every corner of the earth. And finally melted and won, God lovingly works with that heart, continually beckoning and drawing it still closer to Himself until His own life is formed within.

I have no intent here to write a theological treatise. I'm just trying to put some perspective on my quest to understand and embrace His great love, a love that is greater than all my sin. These seedling thoughts began to form within me during that revival. Of course, at the time this was new thinking for me. What I had only grasped in a cursory way was the idea that while God does hate sin, He loves people, and His love-grace is greater than my sin. It is this "greater grace" that was beginning to dawn on me during the fall revival of 1968 under Brother Paul Meigs' ministry.

The foundation that was laid, cultivated, nurtured, and celebrated in the years of my youth has provided bedrock for my faith. These personalities and events that surrounded me and shaped me live in me still as I write now. They have imprinted my soul with the permanent ink of God's stamp on my life. Though I would continue to wrestle with my own failures and with my understanding of God's calling on my life for years to come, I knew that God was calling me and that He wanted a relationship with me. I understood neither. But as the years have rolled by and the seasons have passed, it has proven to be more than a firm foundation. It is the firm foundation that has only grown more firm with time.

CHAPTER 3

The Marines: Lost, but Not So Lost

As a person grows and changes, dreams can also change. Sometimes the change can be huge and obvious to all; other times they are small shifts known only to the dreamer. Some dreams replace others while still more evolve, as doors open and desires grip the soul. And then there are those dreams that rise from the heap of disillusionment, born of frustration with what is, a longing for change, the longing to find a new path. I think all of these reflect what might have motivated me to turn my attention away from a divine call to "preach" and join the Marines Corp.

I was working at Sparky Charcoal in Ocala, living life as a laborer by night and a high school student by day. I enjoyed school but not academia. By my senior year, many friends were planning where they would go to college, busy planning their lives. As I have already mentioned, my grades were nothing special and college was not something to which I had given serious thought. Honestly, I don't remember giving much thought to my future at all.

I was enjoying church and my friendships there throughout high school, especially during my senior year. The choir was very popular and we toured with the cantata, "*I Wonder*," in which I had a solo part. The end of the cantata led into an "altar call" so that people, primarily young people, could be led to make decisions for Christ. Many times, young people would come forward to get "saved" or "rededicate" their lives to the Lord. I remember that quite often during those altar calls I would step to the microphone and make a plea of some kind whenever there seemed to be a waning in responses. Many times God would honor my words and the resultant responses seemed to evidence it. The ironic thing was that while this "ministry" could have confirmed a vocational call of God on my life, it did nothing to move me to pursue it.

I began to watch the evening news during my high school days, particularly my senior year. The Vietnam War was almost always the lead story and I was fascinated with the film clips of warriors engaging enemies. Over a period of time, a fascination and then a desire began to grow. I was young for a senior, seventeen, but I began to think seriously about the military. Gene, my older brother, was in the Air Force already, but for me there was only one branch of the service worth real consideration, the United States Marines.

During the fall of my senior year in high school, I visited a recruiter, took a paper test, and brought home brochures with impressive pictures of marines concealed in camouflage, and, even better, in dress blues with white hat and gloves. I was convinced and told my parents, "I want to join the Marines!" As I say in an earlier writing, "More than anything, when I joined the Marines it was an effort to be awarded the compliment and command of respect. As I grew up, I'd noticed early on that marines were almost revered. I wasn't sure what was required to become one, but I was certain that I wanted the title." Before the winter of 1971 was over, I had made trips to Jacksonville for my physical and been signed into the Marines on a delayed entry program. I graduated high school (my mother's prerequisite before she would sign the papers for her underage son to join the Marines) in June in the top ten percent of the bottom third of my class, and three weeks later reported to Parris Island for basic training.

During my short time in the Marines, I was stationed in South and North Carolina, California, and overseas in the Far East. I rose to the rank of Corporal in less than two years by being meritoriously promoted twice, and eventually shot "expert" having received the best score in my unit. I received several awards and commendations and I was on the fast track in just about every category. I trained with the best and learned warrior's skills which I could use with deadly accuracy. I was tested in every way imaginable and found courageous, though scared out of my wits more than once. I knew great men of impeccable moral character and strong convictions, men worthy of honor and emulation.

I also knew men who could only be called "the others," men of low morals and high alcohol tolerance. Unfortunately, these were the men I chose as friends. At first I fancied myself an evangelist, reading my Bible, going to church, even singing in the choir. But it didn't take long for my Light to dim and darkness to grow. Most of these men were like me: young, right out of high school, cocky, bullet proof, wild, and away from home for the first time in their lives. Many of the struggles in my youth with tobacco and pornography returned with unparalleled intensity in a land of no restraints. I drank freely, cursed fluently, indulged my baser nature relentlessly, and consequentially, my conscience steadily died. My Christian foundation seemed to crumble at every turn. I resisted no temptation and indulged myself as much as my money would allow. The depths of my "fallenness" cannot be overstated or exaggerated. I simply allowed myself every hedonistic pleasure I wanted. I became like the men I spent time with.

That is not to say that the Marines was a terrible experience and that everything I did was bad. While there was a reckless balance to my time there, I experienced the love of comrades under some dire circumstances. I met people and had experiences I cherish, most of which I rarely mention. I saw hope in the face of a child who had no visible reason to hope. I witnessed compassion unlike any I've seen since those days long ago. I've even received the last drop of water from a friend's canteen, freely given to comfort me. So, I don't regret being in the Marines. I cherish it . . . and . . . He was there.

As I recount the litany of my failures here, I intend neither to glamorize nor gloss over them. I am ashamed of and embarrassed by many things to which I willingly gave myself, and my failures were mine alone. I don't blame my Marine brothers with whom I associated for my fall nor do I blame the Marine Corps for my debauchery. The Corps always presented me with the highest ideals in terms of character and honor nor do I blame God for not delivering me from temptation. On the contrary, His faithfulness to me and His love for me were both my constant hope and dread. Any backslider will attest to the presence of "Him with whom we ultimately have to do" in the midst of his sin. I was quite literally a miserable sinner, but my foundation didn't fail me, my Marine brothers did not fail me, and most assuredly, my God did not fail me.

In the darkness and loneliness, the danger and fear, and yes, even in the sin . . . there He was. His light would flicker in me, calling and drawing me back. He would come in unexpected ways and sometimes in profound silence. His presence was as it always is, nonjudgmental and merciful.

There was one such night, while sitting on a hill looking out over a vast canyon to another hill, a moonless, starry night, His presence came to me. His love engulfed me, His peace rested in me. I can see it and feel it at this moment, as it was then. It was real and it was Him, coming toward his prodigal and wondering how long I could stay away. Oh, my heart cried for Him that night and I knew His loving touch as He bore my distresses.

There was a true Christian who worked in our shop and fixed PR-25 radios. He quietly sang the songs of his faith amongst us, and God's light shone from his life to mine. I admired him so for being what I couldn't. He took me to a Pentecostal mission church which lavished me with Father's great love. Oh, how they loved me. The fellowship was rich and reminded me of those times when our youth group would gather around a piano and Cindy Marshall would play, and we would sing. It made me homesick, not for Mom and Dad, but for Father, for Papa. The members of that little church prayed for my strength to be renewed, and I cried deep repentant tears as they laid hands on this Baptist boy and powerfully prayed in known and unknown tongues that this backslider would come back to the fold. They ministered to me, asking God to give me power over the devil and his influences in my life.

There was that morning when the obstacles were too great, the fears too much. He came to me! He came to me that morning and He settled me and made "my feet like hinds feet on high places."

There were the times of danger and uncertainty. He came to me then too. He wasn't loud, but He came to me! He strengthened my nerve and assured my resolve, and I knew it was Him. And there were the times when the burden of my own sin was too heavy. Yes, He even came then too. His love came to me, saying, "Son, I still love you!" He called me son. And He still loved me! He was there and He never failed me.

I remember when I left home in early January, 1972, headed back to California, then to a stint overseas that I had a feeling of dread. I felt I was headed for some scary times. I even felt that I might die and I had a strange sense that I was leaving my home for the last time. Looking back to that year overseas, I think part of me did die. I lost so much that year. I suppose that I, like most people who experience such things, tend to accentuate the adventurous, fun times and push the not-so-good times within and try to move on. I think for the most part I have tried to keep it all in some reasonable perspective, dealing with unpleasant events the way that best fits me.

But as the time came for me to return from a year overseas, I was anxious to see family and friends. I was more than ready to have a month away from the Marines and just relax. I still had more than a year before my first enlistment was scheduled to end, but I sure was glad to be headed "back to the world," as we called it. The many life experiences I encountered in those few months have been part of my soul for all the years since, and as I headed back to CONUS (Continental United States) in early April, 1973, I had a feeling that something was up, that change was coming, and that God was going to revive me and bring me back to a real relationship with Him. Little did I know that He was about to work in ways I could never have imagined.

CHAPTER 4

Love That Will Not Let Me Go

The trip home brought me back to where I left a year earlier, San Francisco, California and Travis Air Force Base. I have chosen to be vague about much of that year because I feel it is outside the purpose of this writing. The long story short is this: by the time the long flight back to the states was over in the spring of 1973, I had determined that I would move forward. Granted, my experiences were nothing when compared to many others, but I have not been trapped by experiences as others have. I adjusted quickly, and have rarely relived that year. Not counting a few unwelcome dreams here and there and that time Bev (my future wife) grabbed my ankle to stop me from crawling under the bed, I have been pretty successful at leaving most of that year where it should be, in the past.

In many ways, I was changed by my experiences. Some of these I have already chronicled. But it seemed to me that the America I had grown up in had changed even more. Many soldiers returning from tours in Vietnam and other places were greeted with jeers. Many were called names and ridiculed. "How many babies did you kill?" Others were spat upon and even attacked. There was a growing "Peace Movement" in the land, but there was hostility on college and university campuses dating back to before I left and seemed only to have intensified in the year I was away. People were burning draft notices and vowing they would not go to war. Returning veterans soon learned to quietly melt back into society unnoticed. It wasn't very popular to have medals from an unpopular war in the late 1960s and early 1970s.

I somehow caught a hop down to Los Angeles International Airport. I felt enough shame and remorse for so many things I had done, and I surely didn't need others to point them out to me or call me names. So once I got there, I hurried into the bathroom, took my uniform off, utilized the trash can to rid myself of offensive signs that I might be one of "those", and crawled into my comfortable "civvies" before I caught a flight the rest of the way home. Of course I didn't know it then, but I would never put that uniform on again.

My sister, Ann, greeted me at the Jacksonville International Airport in Jacksonville, Florida. We rode by her apartment there and then headed on to Ocala to finally see Mom and Dad. I was overjoyed to be home. Wherever I had been that long year, whatever I had done, whatever mistakes I'd made were all somewhere else now. I was "home." Home! The word itself brought such comfort to my soul.

It was early April, 1973, and I had a month off—most of which went by in a blur. I busied myself with visiting friends and reconnecting. I spent time with Don Nelson, one of my best childhood friends. I visited old school teachers, and my dear Aunt Minnie Belle. Ann would come and go, and I loved being with her again. My "second sister", Lynn Barker would come by, and we'd sit and share and laugh just like always. We called her Perky. I've never known anyone who thought about or sought to help others more than Perky. She was in every way important, a real sister to me. I spent time with Momma and Daddy as we'd rock away the evening hours on the front porch. I did whatever I wanted. I bought a used, baby blue, Volkswagen Super Beetle with the help of Daddy's signature. I wanted a car to take me to my next duty station, Camp Lejuene, North Carolina. It had no air conditioning and a pretty basic radio, but it was the newest car I had ever owned and I was truly proud. I went back to Wyomina Park Baptist Church and sang the songs of faith and enjoyed the fresh wind of spiritual renewal. Many of my old friends from church were still around and I loved seeing them. Yes, it sure felt good to be home!

Time went by faster than I wanted. The days slipped away, and I began to both look forward to and dread the time when I would have to leave again. As that time neared, Ann decided that I needed a Welcome Home . . . Good Bye party. She came home from Jacksonville with her friend, Jill. We worked in the yard quite a while to get it presentable for folks to come over and party in the Baptist way of partying. We were hot and tired from the yard work and decided to go to Lake Waldena to swim and cool off before the night's festivities. We climbed into my Super Beetle and laughed and sang our way to the lake—just like so many times before.

We decided to rent a canoe and take a leisurely ride around the lake. At the corner to the right, there was the tree we had jumped from so many times before, and I wanted to give it a whirl. Clad in my tiger stripped shorts left from my time overseas, I climbed the skinny tree. Here's irony: when I was half way up, Ann asked me if I was going to check the depth of the water. I laughed and said, "No! I'm not climbing this tree twice." I performed what I considered the perfect swan dive. Unfortunately, the water level had receded in the almost two years I'd been away. I hit the water; then I hit the bottom. The jolt knocked the breath out of me and stunned me pretty good, but I was not knocked unconscious. I was aware that I had hit the bottom of the lake and I just needed to shake it off and swim to the surface. But when I tried, I couldn't move. I could see the surface but was unable to move toward it. Ann tells that I came up once and then disappeared. As I seemed to dredge the bottom, I began to realize that if I couldn't surface, I'd drown. I felt no panic, but I do remember praying: "Lord, into Thy hands I commit my spirit." And then I drifted off to sleep. I must rely on Ann's recollections to recount what happened next. She writes in third person.

He came up once and his face cleared the water. He came up one other time . . . this time only the back of his head. And then there was no Bill. They waited. Bill almost always swam underwater so the panic came slowly. Finally Ann yelled for him. There was no answer. She yelled again and again and finally said: "Bill, you'd better be hurt because if you're not, I'm going to kill you myself!" And she jumped in the water to look for her little brother.

Ann told Pat (a friend of Ann's from church camp) to call for help. Misunderstanding, Pat started calling Bill's name. Ann stopped her and said "No! Call for help."

Pat did and another canoe came over to help. They pulled their canoe to the small island where the tree was and asked where he went in. Ann had just resurfaced and while holding on to the canoe, she told them—pointing to the area. As she pointed, she looked down and saw that he was beneath her on the bottom.

She dove down again and pulled him to the surface. Pat helped as they lifted him into the canoe . . . well partially into the canoe. He hung over the edge of the canoe, and it was then that Ann lost control. She was screaming and crying and was positive that he was dead. Pat's voice somehow got through to her. "Get in here and help me give him first aid."

As Ann climbed into the canoe she screamed, "I don't know first aid." They paddled their canoe over to the other canoe and the guy helped them get Bill out of the canoe and onto the ground. They turned him over and pumped some water out of him. Twice they did this and then Bill started to breathe. He was alive!

While the guy was turning Bill over, Ann held Bill's head trying to keep his face out of the mud. Now she panicked . . .

"**His neck is broken!"**

"No! He's just in shock."

Bill came to and told Ann not to cry, that he was okay. She calms down and then Bill said, "I can't move!"

As he started to panic, Ann says, "You're alright, you're just in shock. You're moving your foot . . . you're okay."

They went back and forth like this for awhile.

The other canoeists went to the public beach to call for an ambulance. Pat, Ann and the guy (never did learn his name) put Bill in the canoe and the two canoes headed to shore. Once there, the canoe was carried up onto the dry land and they waited for the emergency personnel. They arrived and began to take out the seat and the cross-bars from the canoe.

Pat told Ann that the folks who helped were leaving and Ann went to thank them. She returned and they got into the ambulance to head to the hospital.

I awoke on a stretcher on the shore, was placed into an ambulance and taken to Ocala's only hospital. I remember the ride being short and not much more. Ann remembers that she and I sang on the way. I knew I couldn't move, but I couldn't figure out why. Sometime after we arrived at the hospital, a doctor came by and told me I had broken my neck. This news somehow calmed me. I had broken bones before, my hand and my wrist two times. This was just another broken bone, or so I thought.

Because I was in the military, it was decided that I should be transferred to the Naval Air Station in Jacksonville, so along with my mom I was loaded in an ambulance and taken there. I remember being sleepy and tried to drift off to sleep several times, but the ambulance driver and Mom kept telling me to stay awake. Once there, the Navy doctors examined me, and the next thing I knew I was on the way to St. Vincent's Hospital in downtown Jacksonville. I was placed in traction and roomed in ICU where I stayed for ten days. Somewhere early on, the doctors gave my parents the prognosis: If I lived, I would never walk again, and in the unlikelihood that I did walk, it would only be with the aid of crutches and braces.

During my time in ICU, I'm sure Mom and Dad were there, and Ann came too. I'm told that many family friends made the one hundred mile journey on a number of occasions. I remember but one visitor. I didn't recognize him then and I have no idea who he was. He was a large, bearded man. He spoke to me and then said, "I've come to pray for you." He laid his hands on my chest and prayed in tongues and then thanked the Lord in English for my healing. (I recognized tongues from my experience overseas.) He turned and left quietly. I never saw him again. I've often wondered about this mystery "pray-er." Was he an angel, some sort of vision or "visitation"? Was he a minister who routinely came by the hospital to pray for the sick? Was he a doctor who also believed in prayer? I asked nurses if they knew who the man was, but none could tell me. One thing is for sure, coincidence or supernatural "visitor," soon after he left I was transferred out of ICU and given a semi private room.

I spent three weeks at St. Vincent's. During that time I had surgery to remove bone fragments from my spinal column and an operation that took a bone from my hip and fused it in place of my shattered C4 vertebrate, a fracture so destroyed that I was told it was like dropping a glass plate on the kitchen floor. I was totally paralyzed from the neck down and to add drama to an already horrific injury, I also was suffering from pneumonia. Mom was an angel who sat patiently by my side from early morning until late at night. She would remove mucus from my mouth, hold my hand, and care for my every need. I was fitted with a custom made 4-poster brace that I would wear for months.

One night just before visiting hours ended, as I lay flat on my back, my arms lying on two pillows, I had an urge to try to move my left arm. I labored for quite a while and then it happened. I turned my left arm over. Though the feat fatigued me greatly, sapping all my strength, I was elated at the accomplishment. Remembering that just a few weeks earlier I could run five miles with a forty pound pack, do one hundred pushups and eighteen pull-ups without much effort at all, now it took every ounce of strength and determination I could muster to turn an unwilling hand over. But that night was a huge step and it buoyed my hope that just maybe I would be well. But the progress was painfully slow and would continue to be for weeks and months and years to come. Thankfully, I was blissfully ignorant of the process and effort it would take to make even the slightest improvement.

I began physical therapy soon after I arrived on the ward. It was a slow process. I remember being transferred to a tilt table so that they could gradually angle me to an upright position. The blood rushed to my head and I passed out. But physical therapy, as I would learn, is a long, relentless process. Through many such experiences, many failures and incremental successes, I took my first steps. I'll never forget the first time I saw my upright frame in a full length mirror. I weighed one hundred, twenty four pounds, was clad in short pajamas with a catheter bag at my waist, my right arm in a sling and the ever present 4-poster brace around my neck, a therapist at both my sides. I looked at the skeleton that was me and could barely recognize myself. The fact that I was "up" was amazing, but I was overwhelmed at the scrawny man in the mirror. The ordeal quickly exhausted me and I returned to my room, spent. I asked for a mirror and was given one. My mom held the mirror before my face. I had a scrubby beard (the doctor had advised me to grow the beard to help prevent ingrown hair and provide a cushion for my chin from wearing the brace), my eyes seemed sunk deep into my sockets, and my teeth were almost black from medication. The bullet proof Marine was gone and the shell of a nineteen year old boy was all that was left.

Around this time, two Marines visited me from the Jacksonville area. They looked like I had looked only a short time before. Their uniforms were impeccable, Khaki shirt and tie, blue trousers with a red stripe down the seam, white cover (hat) in their hands. They each carried a briefcase. They asked me how I was doing and made small talk. They were very interested in my story and questioned me about the accident that would change my life. They were polite, but they were also there on business. I don't think I understood then, but I soon learned that the Marine Corps had no place for a person with my prognosis.

About three weeks after the accident, I was transferred back to the Jacksonville Naval Hospital I had been taken to the night of the accident. At St. Vincent's, they had treated me like special royalty. I was in a semi-private room with no other patients. Nurses pampered me and quickly answered my calls. My mom was at my side and cared for my every need. I had many visitors at night and everyone made a big to-do over me. Back at Jacksonville, I was one of many. I was placed into a four-man room on the sixth floor and was kept in my four-poster brace around the clock. I had only worn the brace when I was moved for therapy at St. Vincent's. I contracted a serious urinary tract infection and still had the lingering effects of pneumonia. Mom had gone home and back to work. I learned that I was being medically discharged from the Marines and that I was on a waiting list for a V.A. hospital closer to my home. My dream of being a Marine slipped away in an instant, the only vestige left was the tattooed Bull Dog with the letters "USMC" on my now scrawny, useless right arm. I had no idea what my next move would be. I was ill-equipped to plan for such uncertainties, and I wondered if God Himself had left me.

Ann still came almost every afternoon to see me. As I look back on that time now, I realize how little I appreciated the hardship I placed upon her and my parents. Ann was going to school and working in Jacksonville and Mom and Dad made the trip from Ocala every Sunday. They never seemed to mind the travel and inconvenience my situation placed upon them, and I wish I had told them more how much I appreciated their visits and sacrifices. Later, when I was transferred to Tampa, Mom and Dad still made the trip every Sunday. I've lived long enough now to clearly see my own selfishness, but at the time I was absorbed in my own little world, and it seemed to still be shrinking. I felt alone, and I was depressed.

Physical therapy started in earnest at the naval hospital. Five days a week, twice a day, I was wheeled downstairs to undergo an agonizing routine that stretched and bent my body. My chief therapist was a tall, thin man with a pleasant disposition. He always seemed genuinely glad to see me, and I credit his work, often against my will, for my walking and gradual increased movement during that time. In fact, I must say that all the nurses and therapists I had over the course of the better part of two years were incredible. Well, there was one exception. An unlikeable nurse at the naval hospital discovered that I was an active-duty Marine. Suddenly, I was expected to get rid of the beard that cushioned my chin, change my sheets, and make my bed. She also assigned me some hospital duty. The next thing I knew, I was in the hallway, standing on a chair, right arm in a sling with my walking cane tucked into it, cleaning out a linen closet. Luckily, my doctor came by and saw me. He exclaimed, "What the hell are you doing?"

"The nurse assigned me to clean out the closet, and ordered me to shave my beard," I replied.

Long story short, I never had to clean the closet, nor did I ever see that nurse again. The beard stayed too.

I gained balance and was able to start walking with a cane and a pretty noticeable limp. I rode a stationary bicycle three miles, twice a day, and lifted weights with my legs and arms. Nothing to brag about, no hundred-pound weights, but strength was returning, especially in my legs and left arm. My right arm was not fairing as well. I had no biceps, my wrist wouldn't flex, and I had almost no grip. But overall, I was improving far better than the earlier predictions.

Sometime in mid summer, Ann took me home for a visit. I had graduated from the four-poster brace to a small neck collar and I was more than ready for a break in the monotony of the hospital routine. It was great to be at home, but the heat of our un-air conditioned house fatigued me too much. Though I vowed not to return again until I was discharged for good, the trip enabled me to thank people for their visits and helped me focus on the task at hand . . . getting better.

I made friends in the hospital, and before long I would be the senior patient on the sixth floor, with the dubious honor of the one who had been there the longest. One friend's name was Dave. He was a fellow Marine who had been in a motorcycle accident and broken his leg pretty badly. By the time I met him, he was tooling around in a wheelchair, his leg propped out straight. He was always energetic and optimistic about the future. We began to spend a lot of time together, and he helped lift my spirits considerably. Before I was allowed to walk by myself on the ward, he would come by in his wheelchair, I would latch my wheelchair to his with my cane, and off we would go. (It's hard to steer a wheelchair with one arm. It tends to go in circles.) One time we even left the hospital grounds and wheeled our way to the PX (Post Exchange). He never seemed to tire of hauling me around. At night, when the floor nurse left to serve meds to the floor below us, we'd get in the hall, Dave at one end, me at the other, take out canes and hit my therapy ball back and forth hockey style. He lifted my spirits and I am grateful God placed him in my life at the right time.

Another friend I made was with a guy in the room with me, Tim. An automobile accident left his hands and legs paralyzed. He was in a striker frame that rotated. He spent half the day lying in bed watching TV and the other half flipped onto his stomach facing the floor through a hole in the bed. I never remember him in a wheelchair. He came about a month before I was transferred to Tampa. He had a great sense of humor and was able to laugh at things that happened as he laid there. He never seemed to get down. On days when he received his enema, the stench on the ward, and more particularly, in our room was unbearable. Even then, Tim would make jokes and laugh away the day. His humor and optimism was contagious and was a blessing in my life.

As I was finishing therapy one day, I saw a man in the whirlpool whom I had not seen before. He said hello, and we struck up a conversation. He had been a Prisoner of War in Vietnam since 1967 (five and a half years) and suffered severe injuries to his arms and one leg. During the summer of 1973, he was an outpatient at the naval hospital and came in several times a week. Though he was an officer, he was very friendly and always wanted to know how I was doing. He shared some of his experiences as a prisoner, but mostly he just spoke quietly. I was impressed with his keen wit and easy way, and I found him to be a very affable and articulate man. He would later rise to the rank of Rear Admiral in the Navy, become a U.S. Senator from Arizona, and run for president twice. His "bounce back" rule (learned through the tortures suffered as a Vietnam POW) helped me believe that I too could bounce back. His name was John McCain.

There were others. There was the orderly who took me for a ride down the coastal highway to St. Augustine in his fire-engine-red Mach III Mustang convertible. There was the Gunnery Sergeant who had a broken back who came into my room on a daily basis. He shared stories of his travels and life in the Marines. Though he was concerned about his career-ending injury, he buoyed me with his friendship and openness. These men and others helped lighten my burdens during the months I was in the naval hospital. I didn't know it then, but the Father was trying to show me his love through these friends. His compassion was quietly laid before me, and without His hand using them, I would forever be a bitter, lonely soul. The Father was again rescuing me at a time I couldn't even see Him. I have found that that is one of the ways He does things. He restores from tragedy and calamity, and He does it through people we never expect. Often, the thing that seems the worst possible tragedy turns into a point of praise when He makes things more clear later on. Today, as I write, it is clearer than ever that He was working his grace in me as I was struggling to find myself in the midst of the clamor that was the summer of 1973.

In late September, I was transferred to the V.A. hospital in Tampa. Today, the Spinal Cord Injury Unit is a large separate wing of the hospital, but then it was a small ward of two hallways. I had been "medi-vaced" by plane and arrived in the early evening. I was placed in a room with two men, both paralyzed from the neck down. I soon learned that I was the only one on the entire ward who was ambulatory. I remember feeling badly because I could walk. Despite a noticeable limp and cane and the fact that my right arm was functionally useless, I was a medical wonder and these new roommates marveled at me. We became ready friends and I did whatever I could to help them. I'd light their cigarettes; help them drink water, as we'd talk for hours on end. The routine of physical therapy continued, my ability to walk increased, and I soon lost the cane.

In early October the doctor proposed an operation that would relieve pressure from my spine and might help restore some function in my right arm. The operation was called a laminectomy, a procedure where I would be cut down the back of the neck and "repaired," which included taking out additional bone fragments still lodged in my spinal column. It was a dangerous surgery, I was told, and could leave me permanently paralyzed. After it was done, I had several days of intense pain, but that surgery gave me bicep responses. I turned twenty years old, with a nasty scar on the back of my neck, a shaved back of my head, and an almost immediate increase in bicep movement. It was hailed a success by all. Soon, I was out of the neck collar and continued getting stronger day by day. I walked around the ward several times a day, went to therapy twice a day, and watched a lot of television.

As Thanksgiving approached, I was being readied for release from the hospital. Dad had prepared a table in my bedroom where he rigged the weight slide I would use to continue gaining strength in my right arm. So much had changed for me, and I was keenly aware that the new year would bring more challenges to face and obstacles to overcome. I wasn't "well". I had a long way to go. My limitations worried me. I was self-conscious of the way I looked and walked. I was no longer the Marine who had the world by the tail. But as I was driven from the Spinal Cord Injury Unit that Wednesday, I was excited to be discharged after seven difficult months. I was glad to see 1973 coming to an end. And I was glad to finally be coming home, again.

CHAPTER 5

Of Demons and Angels . . . and God

Christmas time! A year earlier, I was overseas, and Christmas came and went almost unnoticed. No tree. No presents. No caroling. No lights. I had spent that day on guard duty, staring out into the wooded darkness in case there was trouble. But after a long year away and after so much had transpired, I was home again, and it was Christmas. I had the money to buy my family presents, but so much more important, I was home. As a new year arrived, I readied myself for the challenges of being "disabled." To say the New Year would be a rocky year would be a gross understatement. 1974 would be long, painful, and difficult.

My first order of business was to buy a car. Dad had returned my baby blue Volkswagen because it had a standard transmission. I took him with me to the Pontiac dealership and fell in love with a brand new maroon Firebird Formula 400. Though my dad "wouldn't have it," it was the car for me! I was so proud and immediately began driving it like crazy. It was automatic, the only option that was a must since I couldn't use my right hand to shift gears. For the first time in a long time, I felt like "somebody!"

I didn't know it then, but my routine for the next year and a half would be to go to the V.A. hospital in Tampa three times a week for physical therapy. I discovered early on that the trip to Tampa was far more draining than I could ever have imagined. I journeyed Monday, Wednesday, and Friday, and it took all the other days of the week to recover from making the agonizing trips each of those three days.

The schedule was grueling. I was exhausted almost all the time. My therapy was basically checking the progress of my home therapy and adding new exercises to strengthen my right arm which was still almost nonfunctional. I'd lift weights with my legs, paying extra attention to my right. Even so, my limp was more than noticeable and I walked with a gait that embarrassed me. As always, the stretching exercises were not only tiring but painful as well. At the end of therapy, I'd gather my frame into the Firebird and head back to Ocala. In all, I'd spend about six hours per visit traveling and exercising.

On my off days, I found it almost impossible to get out of bed in the mornings. I became a "soap opera" junky and slumped into an unproductive routine. Many days I wouldn't get up until two in the afternoon. I rarely tried to make my bed. I would half heartedly do my strength exercises and not much else. By late afternoon, I would begin dreading the next day's trip back to Tampa.

Small daily tasks frustrated me. Simple things like buttoning a shirt or taking a shower added to my exhaustion. I struggled with learning to feed myself left handed and I was still trying to figure out how to write legibly. I smoked cigarettes like they were going out of style and generally felt worthless. I became depressed and saw no light at the end of the tunnel, even though I had already made so much progress and surpassed the highest expectations of the doctors who had originally diagnosed me.

Depression is an interesting phenomenon. I suppose we have all experienced it to some extent. For me, it was a gradual emotion that wanted to trump all others. I was alone a lot and had a hard time shutting my mind off. I took stock of what I no longer had, and it preyed upon me that I would never be "normal." The Bible has a verse that describes my disposition during the first half of 1974. "Your adversary, the devil, prowls around like a roaring lion, seeking to devour" (1 Peter 5:8). And he was winning. He roared about all I had lost and he was both proficient and consistent. He'd seem to highlight my short comings and downplay any small accomplishment. And he seemed to know exactly which buttons to push as my emotional state continued to descend. He was an expert at pointing out that I wasn't a Marine, that I would never find a girl who would want to marry a "cripple," that I'd never be smart enough to accomplish anything, that I looked stupid with my limp and worthless arm, that I'd never be able to take care of myself, that I was a burden on my parents though they never said so to me, that people were laughing at my grotesque figure behind my back, that the world would be better off without me, that in fact it would have been better for everyone had I drowned in that lake . . . and a thousand more "that's."

Sometime early in the year, I decided to try to get a job. The adversary was careful to let me know that no one would hire such a worthless excuse for a "man" as I. But as I looked through the want ads one day, I found an ad looking for disabled veterans. I didn't consider myself much of a veteran, but I was painfully aware that I was "disabled." I went to see if there was a job I could do. As I walked into the small office, a man greeted me, and we began to chat. He told me he was marketing a product that was amazing: A light bulb that would never burn out. In fact, he said, it was indestructible and unbreakable. To prove the point, he said he could throw it against the wall and it wouldn't break. To convince me further, he did just that. He threw a bulb against the wall. It broke into a million pieces. Embarrassed that I had even come in, I walked out. There to meet me and walk back to the car with me was the adversary. "You can't even get a job selling stupid light bulbs."

That "stupid light bulb" was a metaphor for me. I had once been an amazing product, indestructible and unbreakable. I, too, had been thrown against the wall and shattered, broken into a million pieces. That light bulb, like Humpty Dumpy, would never be able to be put back together, and neither would I. Sure, I might get a little better, I might gain a few movements, I might even one day look almost normal. But I'd never be of any more value than that destroyed light bulb. The words both whispered and screamed in my ears had finally entered my heart and I believed them. I was worthless and always would be. I had arrived at a new, all time low.

For the first time I seriously considered suicide. I had thought about it before, but had always quickly dismissed it from my mind. Now, it took root and was a constant in my small world. Surely the world would be a better place if there were one less "cripple" around. My dad owned a .22 rifle and I was an expert marksman, trained while in the Marines to accurately fire a variety of weapons. I had all the symptoms too: I had a plan, the means, the motive, but did I have the will? For those who have never felt this depth of worthlessness and hopelessness, or never heard the pounding words of the adversary condemning your every thought or deed, it's hard; no, it's impossible to describe. But I felt it and heard it at every turn. I thought my demise would free my family from caring for their disabled son. I thought it would bring an end to my tormented mind. I thought it would end my pain and loneliness. As I write these words now, years removed from the passion of that long ago time, I see how selfish, how self-absorbed and hollow these thoughts were, but at the time day after day, they were a steady partner beating a drum that drove me on. I'd rather not go into further detail, but it is important for you to know that that was a very dark time and the shadows that surrounded me were constant. Of course, anyone looking in might have missed the turmoil raging within me. I had a cool new car. I had money for the first time in my life thanks to "disability" checks. I bought nice suits and just about anything else I wanted. But inside, a real battle was raging. A malicious, determined adversary prowled; I was facing a giant and the giant was winning.

. . . But God . . . .

"**But God,** being rich in mercy, because of the great love with which He loved (me)" (Eph. 2:4). "I was sinking deep in sin, far from the peaceful shore. Very deeply stained within, sinking to rise no more. But the Master of the sea, heard my despairing cry, from the waters lifted me, now safe am I. Love lifted me . . . When nothing else could help, love lifted me" (Love Lifted Me, *Broadman Hymnal*, James Rowe, 1912).

God's love comes in an infinite variety of ways and it came to me. I didn't even recognize it at the time. He used people as instruments of His work, and I must mention two "angels" in particular that He sent me in my darkest time. One was Don Nelson. I had known Don since high school and he was a treasured and trusted friend. I'm not sure exactly when or how it happened, but he started coming around. He thought I needed to learn the game of tennis. He took me to our town courts and slowly and patiently began teaching me the game. At the time, my right arm was little more than a dangling nuisance and my right leg showed an embarrassing limp, but none of that phased Don. He had survived a brain tumor himself, and he didn't "do" the word "quit." He'd open the tennis ball can with a "whoosh" and then say, "You know what that sound is? That's the sound of me opening a can of whoop ass on you." With that, he'd laugh and so would I. I'd hit the ball erratically, and Don would chase my errant shots with humor and light-hearted banter. Often, I would trip over my lazy leg and end up on the court, scratched in body and spirit. He'd come running, make sure I was OK and laugh and joke me back to trying again. We'd be on the courts for hours, often the last ones to leave when the lights went out. We'd ride to the convenience store and take turns buying an "RC cola and moon pie." He took me tubing on Rainbow River. He'd call and come by to sit with me on the porch at home. He was a "friend who stuck closer than a brother" as the months of my rehab lumbered on. He never made any claims to be Christian. He didn't consider himself a "follower of Christ." But follower or no, he was chosen by the Father to be His hands extended to His child who had profoundly lost his way.

The other angel I must mention here was my life-long friend, Lynn "Perky" Barker (Jansen). Perky had been like a second sister to me over many years. She was two years behind me in school, and by the time I was out of the hospital, she was in college. She came by every afternoon on her way home from classes, often awakening me from my two o'clock slumbers. I'd drag myself from bed and she would stay and keep me company, and we'd laugh together for much of the afternoon. She later introduced me to some of her friends who were scuba divers, and before long, they had me scuba diving with them. Sometimes Perky would come over in the evening, and we'd talk well into the night. She selflessly allowed me to drone on about whatever I wanted to talk about, rarely concerned for her own trials, always focused on me. It was Perky who talked me into giving college a try and we even had a class in comparative religions together (until I made a nineteen on the first test and dropped the course). Perky was "God with skin" for me during a time when He felt so far away.

What neither of these ambassadors did do, was try to convert, change, or condemn me. Prayer was never offered, and spiritual counsel was never given. They accepted me as I was, where I was and seemed content to be who they were. But they both were "ambassadors for Christ, as though God was making an appeal through (them) . . . Be reconciled to God" (2 Cor. 5:20). One was a doubting agnostic, the other was a true Christian, but both were ambassadors of Father. What they did for me, pulling me out of the miry clay, was nothing short of miraculous, and by summer, I was better physically, emotionally, and spiritually. I was poised for a fresh beginning, not knowing what that might mean. I am forever in their debt for the lift they gave this soul, and I am amazed at a God who can do all things Himself but likes to clothe Himself in rags and sneak in, masked in people's skin, some of whom even deny His very existence.

In the spring, on some of my many trips to Tampa, I began driving to Wauchula to visit my former pastor, Cooper Marshall. He had moved there the summer I left for the Marines. I'd spend the night on Sunday night with him and his wife, Margaret, and then head to Tampa for my Monday therapy appointments. Like Perky and Don, this wonderful couple loved me despite my struggles, and Brother Marshall invited me to do some visiting for him with another young man. We'd visit young people mostly, but it felt great to be doing something that had meaning.

In Ocala, I became more active and intentional in my church participation during the summer. For some reason, I felt ready to attend some functions and started attending the College & Career Sunday school class. I found it boring and uninspiring, but it seemed to be good for my soul. I enjoyed the sound, biblical preaching of Pastor Ernest Walker that summer. He was a graduate of Baptist Bible Institute in Graceville, Florida and had an amazing way of explaining texts that made them interesting and alive.

One night after church, a Thursday night, I sat in my car, alone, as everyone left after a youth service. As I sat there, I rehearsed all that had taken place since that fateful day when I broke my neck. I remembered all the love shown me through that experience. I remembered the depth of my despair that was now lifting more each day, and for the first time in a very long time, I was grateful. As I sat in the car, taking stock of the past year, rain began to fall, and so did the tears, slowly at first, and then deep sobs began to billow from somewhere in my soul. The release that I needed so badly had finally come, and that night I felt new again. In the darkness, I sat and my heart broke. Waves of spiritual emotion ebbed and then ebbed again. Like an epiphany, I realized that while I still had a long way to go, my life would be taking me in a new, unknown direction. Yes, I had a limp. Yes, my right arm was never going to be what it had been. But I could walk. I wasn't in a wheelchair; I didn't have braces on my legs. And I had to admit that a noticeable miracle had taken place, and I realized that God had done something. I found myself overwhelmed that the God I had known and left behind, had known me and never left my side. That night I raised my hand to Him and thanked Him for His amazing grace and care. That night I admitted to God that I was a broken person and that I could not heal my brokenness alone. And I realized for this first time that my brokenness was not physical. It was spiritual. In that very moment, from somewhere within, a scripture came to me. "I have broken but I will heal," says the Lord. (Hosea 6:1, *paraphrase mine*) That night, a change began, and though I would often feel overwhelmed, I knew for sure that He was working His will in my heart and in my life. That night, the constant voice of my adversary, who had preyed on me and almost won, yielded to the God who was greater, and I surrendered to Him as if for the first time. I can't explain that night, even writing now, words won't come, but that night, He, God of The Bible became my Lord. I would be His. Self doubt was still present, but so was He. My future was as uncertain as ever, but He was certain. That night, I was converted and I began a new walk—a new path. I was changed that night. I would live for Him.

In the fall I began college. It was more an aimless attempt to do something with myself. I had no real educational goals in mind, no real direction; it just seemed the thing to do. Business courses were on the agenda, and as always, school was hard for me. I scheduled all my classes in the morning so I could continue to make my therapy sessions three days a week. There were no serious advisors or guidance like there is today, so I just sort of followed the prescribed plan laid out in the Central Florida catalog. My dismal performance in high school came back to haunt me as I began with a remedial prerequisite math class to prepare me for "real" math classes later. On the days I didn't go to Tampa, I'd stay in the library on campus and study. I put myself on a work schedule as though it were my job, studying until five o'clock in the afternoon. I continued to play tennis with Don and would scuba dive with friends, and I tried to ignore the loneliness deep within. On the college campus, I was painfully aware that I looked different from my classmates. My right arm made me self-conscious, so I mostly wore long sleeve shirts, and I still sported a noticeable limp. But my spiritual life was thriving even amidst great struggles. My sister Ann was back in Ocala attending CFCC (now CCF), and I loved that she was close by. Perky and several of her friends babied me and made a big to-do over me to help me fit in. I attended church regularly and was enjoying being there. I'd sit with Mom and Ann, and I remember experiencing great joy as we sang the familiar songs from the Baptist hymnal we all loved so much. But the reality was that I felt like I was merely marking time, waiting for something to catch my attention and captivate my heart. It was in one of those Sunday services when something did just that.

December 4th was that day. The pastor had begun his morning sermon when an unusual thing happened. As I sat, I was suddenly aware that I could see the pastor's mouth moving, but I couldn't hear his voice. It was as if a gigantic soundproof glass had been placed over me, and I was all alone. But I was most definitely not alone. I felt His presence, and He had come to do business with His son. He spoke to my heart as I sat unaware of anyone else. His message was unmistakably clear, and it felt almost audible, and it shook me deep within. "I have called you. I called you years ago, and now I am calling you again. Surrender yourself to me. But if you choose not to, I will not deal with you again."

I was startled. In my mind I wondered, "You will not deal with me again? What does that mean?"

He did not clarify His words, and they unsettled me to the core. While I couldn't know what He meant, I certainly knew He was serious. My mind raced, and memories came flooding back. I remembered that day when I thought I might die on the way to the hospital after being hit by the motor boat. I remembered Brother Marshall's words about preparing myself for ministry when I was so young. I remembered God using me to speak as I gave my testimony or urged the audience to respond to the call of the Father when our youth group went on tour with the musical, *"I Wonder."* And I remembered my failures and my wayward heart, the times I had given myself to sin and let the God of my youth down. Like Peter of the Bible, I had denied I ever knew Him. But now, in the quiet of that Sunday morning, it was decision time for me. He had given me an open invitation and a clear ultimatum . . . I surrendered. What else could I do?

As suddenly as it all had begun, the glass that had encapsulated me lifted. The congregation stood and began singing the old hymn, *"I Surrender All"* which began, "All to Jesus I surrender, all to Him I freely give. I will ever love and trust Him, in His presence daily live." As the verses went by, I hesitated. But the truth was that I had already surrendered. With my feet on auto pilot, I stepped forward and made my surrender public. "God has called me to preach!" I exclaimed. "I am called to the ministry." My profession pleased the assemblage and "Amen's" resounded through the sanctuary of my little home church. I think I intuitively knew that my life was now surely in God's hands, and I would not turn back. A course was set that day, and I felt relieved and clean. I didn't know the next step to take yet, but I had said the big "Yes!" And that "yes" would take care of all the other yeses that would comprise my future. I was on the path to His heart, and I had the purpose for which I had long sought. I wanted to leap as I left the service that day. Well wishers embraced me. Mother cried tears of joy and pride that her son had come finally home, not just home from the Marines, not just home from near death or a long physical ordeal. Her son had come Home; Home to the Father. Indeed I had!

CHAPTER 6

The Bridge to Somewhere

The New Year started with an excited boredom. So much had happened the year before: my reconciliation with the Father and commitment to His call. I felt so excited about the future, generally, except anything that didn't have to do with Him bored me. He had rescued me from myself, given me purpose, and I felt as if He was setting me on His course for the first time. I wasn't sure what that might mean, but I was ready for it. So much was uncertain, but He had captivated me, and nothing less than His fullness would do for me anymore.

I was uninterested in college, but I started the spring semester with a full slate of core classes and a hope that further direction was coming. Try as I would, I was an average student at best and struggled mightily to earn even that academic rating. My sister Ann had enjoyed a professor, Mr. Flemming, who taught in the humanities, and it was she who convinced me to take his speech class. The eight o'clock class fit right into my morning schedule, and I looked forward to honing my speaking skills for someday, out in the future, when I would stand before thousands to preach. The other courses that semester are a blur now. I will describe more about the life-changing event brought about by this course later. My constant passion was Jesus, and I was interested in nothing more than getting busy answering His call on my life.

Ernest Walker was now the pastor of my home church, and as I said earlier, he had graduated from Baptist Bible Institute. He was an amazing preacher, and I assumed his preaching talent came from learning to preach at BBI. It would be a few years before I would comprehend spiritual gifts in any meaningful way, and I had no knowledge at the time that what Brother Walker had was a spiritual gift of teaching. He taught more than he preached, but in the Baptist tradition, these two seemed to be almost synonymous and were used interchangeably. I began talking to him and discovered that BBI was a three-year program of theological and pastoral study that required no college. I had turned twenty-one in October, and that made me eligible to enter. With Brother Walker's help, I filled out applications and readied myself to go as soon as I could. The greatest lure and appeal was that BBI would be an educational shortcut to becoming a preacher. It seemed like the perfect fit for a guy who hated school and was majoring in "Getting Out as Fast as Possible," and if there ever was such a guy, I was he. I made plans to attend BBI the coming fall. I just had to endure one more semester of courses that seemed irrelevant and counterproductive to His divine call on my life. (Again, it would be several years before I could grasp the importance of education generally, its value for church work particularly, or its richness in life and faith especially.)

During that long semester, I had many opportunities to preach: I became a vital part of the Marion Baptist Associational Youth Rallies, and often filled in for small churches when they needed a preacher for a day or a service. My schedule seemed busy, attending a full array of college classes, preaching quite often, my trips for therapy in Tampa, and studying like crazy to maintain my average-student status.

I had changed my dismal habit of sleeping until noon about the time the spiritual light had turned on the summer before. Now, I was accustomed to rising from sleep around five and spending time in prayer and Bible reading, followed by going over class notes and preparing for the day. I was in class at least fifteen minutes early so I could review yet again before Mr. Flemming arrived. I was meticulous in my preparations for all classes, but especially for speech because in that course I saw a direct relevance for my future, perhaps becoming the next Billy Graham or John Calvin. It was early in the new semester, and in that very class that I was surprised with an addition to my already full schedule, one that would change my life.

I'm not exactly sure the first time I noticed her, but notice her I did! She had scheduled the same speech class for eight o'clock in the morning with Mr. Flemming. She bounded in at the last possible moment. She wore little makeup and to be honest, always seemed a little disheveled to me. She sat in the back of the classroom. But as she "whooshed" by me, I found myself drawn to this girl, so much my opposite.

She carried herself comfortably and reminded me of a throwback hippie type with her bellbottoms, sandals, and hip huggers. She was a free spirit, and she owned a sparkle that was hard to ignore! Her dark eyes seemed to dance the dance of life and she always had a smile and ready laugh. There was a charisma about her, a dynamic that made her fun, appealing, and friendly. I can't exactly pinpoint what appealed to me the most or what specific quality rose above the rest, but I was smitten almost immediately. Mr. Flemming didn't call a roll, and I was naturally shy, so it wasn't easy to get an introduction. I finally gathered my nerve and asked someone about her, and at last I found out her name, Beverly "Bev" Cotton.

We began with casual conversations as we walked from class each day. I had talked in a "How to" speech about quitting smoking and being a Christian (a taboo remark in Flemming's class). We'd chat about the speeches coming up and how we would leave Christ out of them because Flemming didn't want testimonials for speech topics. Before long I had invited her out to breakfast after class. This required my skipping my second period Human Relations class on a regular basis, a sacrifice I willingly made. As time passed, we began to share pieces of our walk with the Lord and were amazed how we each felt about Him and serving Him. Bev shared her faith with me as easily as breathing, how she had been saved in high school, after she at last found someone who was a true Christian. She explained an experience she called the baptism in the Holy Spirit, a phrase that was both new to me and which, I must confess, was somewhat scary to me. I was Baptist and I had a lifetime of teaching about salvation and submission to the Lordship of Christ. It made me uncomfortable for this former Methodist to instruct me about the rudiments of biblical teaching concerning the Holy Spirit and His workings. Really, who'd she think she was? Even so, I couldn't deny that she possessed a gentle boldness and genuine openness that I did not.

I say we were opposites, but only in the way we expressed ourselves to the world. We also had many similarities. She came from a good family that practiced the same moral code as my own. We were both athletic and enjoyed sports. We were both spontaneous and enjoyed deciding to do something on the spur of the moment. But far more important than these, we both were passionate Christians who had come out of darkness and into His marvelous light. We both had experienced tragedies that though different had mellowed and changed us. We both loved to read the Bible and discuss insights we were gaining by spending time with Papa. Our early talks were not about theology or denominationalism, but the quality of our relationship with Jesus. So, while it's true that our personalities seemed irreconcilable, the truth was we weren't so different in the ways that really mattered.

At first, this new relationship was based more on a mutual attraction to Christ than each other. I think we were both excited about connecting with someone whose passion for the Father was at least as strong as our own. We'd talk for hours, and I knew that in Bev I had found a kindred spirit. She challenged my thinking and I challenged hers. We discussed the Bible hours on end and wondered what God wanted from our lives. Of course it didn't take long for our spiritual relationship to make room for a personal relationship as well.

As March approached, Flemming encouraged his speech class to attend the college drama's production of the play *Guys and Dolls*. He seemed to think it was worth our while, but I don't remember a grade associated with our attendance. As Bev and I talked I told her, half joking, that since we had to go to the play anyway we may as well go together. To my surprise she liked the idea. We set the "date" and I began to make plans. We'd go to the 1890 House, an elegant and quaint restaurant known for its ambiance and food, for dinner and then to the play. The date was March 8, 1975.

We dressed up for the occasion. Bev wore a black velvet pant suit and looked amazing. She ordered wine, a drink that surprised me. I was now a real Baptist, no alcohol for me; I had sweet tea, a staple drink for me after long training from my mama. We attended the play, making sure Flemming saw us there, and then I took her home. We sat in her front yard and talked as always, and then we kissed. I'm not sure that sparks flew, but emotions did run high for me. It had been quite a while since I had felt such acceptance from a girl and in that moment I saw her in a new light. Before leaving that night I had set up another date a week later. On the drive home that night, I did what I seem to always do, even to this very moment now. I wondered what Papa was up to, and I hoped He was up to something good. A friendship that had started as a spiritual odyssey, two believers hungry for fellowship and someone with whom to share their faith, was now that and something more. Our relationship had begun.

As time moved toward the summer break, Bev and I had grown very close. We enjoyed scuba diving together, took short trips, and we even drove to Hattiesburg, Mississippi to see my brother Gene and his wife, Joan. Gene was attending William Carey College there. While in the Air Force, Gene had experienced "the baptism in the Holy Spirit" as it was called, and he and Bev fed off each other as they jabbered about what God was doing and how He was moving in their lives. I felt a little like the man on deck at a baseball game who was replaced by the coach's son. They were speaking of things I had never really considered and which were not part of my theological repertoire. They called themselves "Charismatic," a term, to be honest, about which I knew nothing. I felt a little left out of the conversation. Actually, I felt a lot left out, and I remember thinking that I didn't think I was supposed to approve of this "second work" of grace stuff. But I couldn't deny that they seemed to have something real that I didn't have.

Back home, Bev and I talked about this second work of grace quite a bit. She was the teacher, and I was the student. I trusted her to help me understand, though I was uncomfortable. At the same time, I hungered for what she was talking about and didn't have a clue how to move beyond what I had always practiced. I knew both intuitively as well as from personal experiences that God was active in the affairs of my life. I was a student of the Bible and believed strongly in the Holy Spirit's workings. It wasn't that I wanted an experience as much as I wanted more of God's life in mine.

One particular night as we sat in the car in front of her house, Bev wanted to pray for me to "receive the Holy Spirit" and speak in tongues. My theology knew I had already received the Holy Spirit, but tongues were another thing. As we prayed she coached me to mutter a few sounds. It wasn't much to be sure, and I felt no tingles, but I became open to the possibility that God wanted me to go deeper in Him. I was in pursuit of the Father, and I would not be idle in that pursuit, whatever it might mean.

Bev attended a coffee house called The Word where young people gathered to sing, and pray, and study the Bible. She dragged me along, and I enjoyed the lively spirit and the solid teaching that was offered. I made friends there, some of whom are still a part of our lives. I loved the songs, so personal, so rich. People didn't sing about the Lord, they sang to the Lord. I had never experienced that. The fellowship was rich and meaningful, and though I was still a bit uncomfortable with some things, I felt His divine presence and rest there.

With the approaching summer, Brother Walker let me know that there was a church in Marathon, Florida, in the Florida Keys, that needed an interim pastor and asked if I was interested. I was indeed. It was a confirmation to me that God was calling me to preach. Though that opportunity didn't pan out, I worked a few weeks at a youth camp as a counselor, and out of that experience had several offers to preach.

At the same time, I knew that I was in love with Bev and wanted to marry her. Her grandfather passed away in June and on the way home from the funeral, somehow we became engaged. We were so excited. We decided on a December wedding and set the date for the 27th. A friend at BBI called me about a mobile home in Graceville, Florida for sale. We drove up and bought it. It wasn't much, but we agreed that it was God's provision and we could afford the sixty-two dollars a month payment. I moved into it to start school while Bev stayed in Ocala to work while we waited to get married at the end of the year. The fall semester started; I studied like crazy, missed Bev like crazy, and could barely stand the separation. We were married at Grace Episcopal Church in Ocala on December 27, 1975. Bev sang the song "*Let us Climb the Hill Together*, by Paul Clark and I recited a writing that I felt God had given me early on in our relationship. In part it said,

"And God said, 'Do you dare not love that which I have given you?'

But I said, 'We are so different!'

But God said, "This is what will make her special to you. She will love you and care for you. She will encourage and strengthen your heart. She will become for you a joy and your love will only grow stronger as time passes."

We spent a few days "honeymooning" and then packed up and headed to BBI to begin married life and all the surprises that lay ahead. We were in love, happy, and in God's plan. He was our Lord and God, the One who had brought us together. Our new life was to be lived for Him. What could go wrong?

CHAPTER 7

New Wine for Old

Bev and I returned to Graceville and our mobile home. It was located on what Bev and I laughingly called "Baptist Row" since almost everyone on that dead end dirt road was Baptist and most attended BBI. I started my second semester of school, and Bev set up housekeeping. The place needed a woman's touch for sure. No pictures adorned the walls, the furniture was "trailer quality," and the black vinyl couch (with matching chair) in the living room rocked when we sat on it. The mattress on the bed caved to the center when we lay down. The dinette set was cheap, too. Bev somehow acquired a huge picture of Jesus that covered one entire wall of the twelve by fifty-two foot dwelling and it was both physically and metaphorically the focal point of our home. It was a humble start, especially looking back now, but for us it was perfect. This was our castle, and we were together at last.

I quickly fell back into my routine. I attended classes in the morning and studied in the afternoon. I had survived a tough and lackluster semester, learning about the inter-biblical period, writing my very first real essay (on which I scored a "D"), and a course in Old Testament. Good grades as always were hard to get, though I studied relentlessly. But the new semester brought very interesting and inspiring classes, my favorite which was Dr. Allen's, Synoptic Gospels class. Dr. Allen was a great professor who passionately shared from his deep study and own spiritual hunger. He had done his doctoral studies on the life of the Apostle John, and he rarely was able to convey a story about him that failed to make him weep. His love of the scriptures fueled my own, and I found his class inspiring and emotional; I enjoyed walking into his class to learn and feel God's holy presence each day.

I didn't just want to be a preacher. I wanted to be a Christian. I wanted to know the Father and please and obey Him. So much of biblical studies can be clinical, sterile, and void of emotion and life. I was far too hungry at this stage of my pilgrimage to settle for mere facts and figures. I had learned from Bev that knowledge without passion could at best produce religion and obedience, but a dynamic relationship with Jesus was what shaped life and joy. I wanted both.

We attended several Baptist churches right off the bat. I have always loved the hymns sung there and I felt His presence through the preaching and song services that the corporate worship services offered. We failed to get deeply involved in any one church, but often visited small churches where friends of mine from school served as pastors. Bev wanted more of the charismatic choruses she had learned and enjoyed at The Word and other experiences from her Open Bible (a Bible college she had attended before we met) days. It didn't take long for a tear in our relationship to emerge. Though we loved each other and the Lord deeply, we weren't on the same page about church or worship. It bothered us both, and it became the huge, invisible, elephant in the corner of our relationship. We both knew it was there but rarely discussed it out loud. The rip only intensified as time passed, and we both became miserable. I would leave for school, go to the chapel and pray, and remember my love for Bev and reflect on how God had brought us together. I would fortify myself to go home and love Bev as in our courtship days. While I was at school, Bev would do much the same thing. She loved me and knew that God had put us together. She'd pray and ask Him to restore the joy we had known only a few weeks before.

We both remember those days well. We have described it as a spirit that seemed to contaminate our relationship and sabotage the joy we should have known as newlyweds. It was like a spiritual humidity within our castle, and it was palpable and it was physical; we could actually feel its presence. When I came home, one of us had to leave the house, go for a walk, and get away from the other. For me, this resulted in seriously questioning my decision to marry; this only a few weeks after the wedding. Once I asked a fellow student who had also gotten married over Christmas break how he liked married life. His enthusiastic response was as it should be, saying, "Man, it's wonderful!" I grinned sheepishly and walked away, becoming more convinced as the days went by that I may have made a huge mistake, perhaps the biggest of my young life.

That is not to say that every moment was that way. We had many joyous times too. We'd take walks together or head to the mall in Dothan, twenty miles away. We'd ride the back roads and explore and enjoy the rural countryside. We'd meet friends and have a great time laughing and talking well into the night. But there was an unmistakable strain in our relationship that was alien in our past experience together, and it held us in a choke hold.

While those days were painful and full of uncertainty, I believe that time was formative as we tried to work through our spiritual differences and form our own identity as a couple. Beverly was very outgoing and I felt threatened to some extent by her charm and joyful personality. It pains me to even say that, but the truth is that her relationship with Jesus was purer and richer than was mine. My relationship with Jesus was far more structured and clinical. I didn't have much spiritual emotion, and what I did have was not based in the Father's pleasure with me, but my place as servant to Him. While I understood that I was His servant, then and always, I had not yet learned of a "son-ship" relationship with a loving heavenly Father. In fact, that revelation would not come for several decades. Bev already knew a deep intimacy with the Savior and her spiritual life was like breathing. Mine was more like breathing through a snorkel and hoping water wouldn't choke me.

As the spring semester at BBI wound down, we decided to see if we could stay in Ocala for the summer. There was a little house next to Bev's parents', a one bedroom bungalow that was perfect for a couple newly married. Arrangements were made, and as soon as school was out, we headed to Ocala. I made arrangements to lead church services at Silver Glenn Springs, a beautiful spring and camping area about forty miles east of Ocala, and we were allowed to camp there every weekend, which we loved. Every Saturday afternoon, I'd go from campsite to campsite inviting campers to attend the 10:00 a.m. church service the next day. Bev would play guitar and lead some choruses, and I'd bring a short devotion with the campers who chose to attend. It wasn't the Welch Revival, but we enjoyed sharing with the strangers and families who came.

The summer in Ocala also gave us time with our parents. The 1976 summer Olympics were taking place, and every night after dinner, we'd make our way next door to watch Sugar Ray Leonard box his way to a gold medal. Jim (Bev's father) and I would go fishing quite a bit that summer too. I got to know my father-in-law better and grew to appreciate his character. The summer passed quickly as summers often do, and before we were ready, it was time to head back to BBI for my second year.

I think we both were ready to get back on our own after a restful break. I knew I would have harder courses and long study hours as I tackled such classes as the Major Prophets and Pauline Epistles. I wasn't real excited, but I was ready to get started. We quickly renewed old friendships from my first year and picked up where we had left off. The summer had given us a sweet reprieve from a difficult spring. We had seemed to make good progress in our relationship and the fall brought a freshness of spirit to us both. We still had to work on what church we'd attend and on how to make Bev into a Baptist preacher's wife with all the accoutrements that would entail. She didn't easily fit into a mold, as any of her friends will confirm. But we were in love, she wanted to be the wife I needed, and we both knew we had a call from God that would somehow bring us through.

Shortly after school began, I saw a friend of mine from my first year. Rip had not been to school the first week or so of the new term, and when I saw him I asked him about that. He told me that he had been filled with the Spirit over the summer and that he was not returning to BBI. I put on my best front and wished him well, but I had not yet gained any real understanding of what it meant to be "filled with the Spirit" though Bev and I had talked at length about this very thing. He said that he and his wife were attending a little charismatic store-front church in Marianna, about twenty miles from Graceville, called Maranatha Christian Center. He said they met on Tuesday night, not Sunday, and invited Bev and I to attend. Honestly, I felt the woolies! But this was the kind of church Bev would surely like and since it met on Tuesday night, it wouldn't interfere with "real" church services like the Baptists have. When I got home that evening, I told her about Rip and this Charismatic church.

I remember the look on her face as though it were yesterday. It was like a hope! I knew that Bev wanted, no, needed to attend this church. I could see it in her eyes; her face had the appearance of a light removing a dark cloud from not just her countenance, but her spirit as well. She asked, though she need not, if she could go. I said yes, but what else could I say? I was afraid, I'm embarrassed to say, that she would find another love, not a man, but a love that would replace me as her joy.

She attended that very night. I was home studying, going to the library to work on the ever present collateral readings required in theological studies. I went home to an empty house and waited for Bev to return, figuring she would beg me to start attending with her. I had my response in hand. I would tell her that I was going to be a preacher in the Baptist denomination and that it would not be appropriate for me to attend a nondenominational church, let alone one with charismatic leanings, that she could go on Tuesday nights if she wanted, but that I wouldn't.

She came home refreshed and alive, but to my surprise she made no request regarding my attendance. She disarmed my philosophical argument before I had a chance to let her know how it was going to be. She did not push; she didn't even nudge. She was just happy that she was able to go and that she enjoyed it very much. Then she told me that the coming weekend they were having a retreat and asked if I'd mind if she went.

It's happened several times in my life: A feeling, an intuition, a divine moment when I knew something secret. I can't say how I knew; I just knew I needed to go to that retreat. My mind was screaming, but I knew, as surely as I've ever known anything, that I simply had to go on that retreat. It was the Father calling me, and my spirit would not have rest until I yielded. Even so, I opened my mouth to say, "Sure, you go ahead." But what I heard myself say was, "Yes, and I want to go too."

It was so unlike me, a shy, somewhat recluse who hated new environs or groups. I wasn't comfortable meeting new people and I had a thousand questions rolling over in my head, but there was no question that I would be at that retreat just three days hence. I prepared myself as best I could. I prayed for God's will, I prayed for guidance, deliverance, even illness. The interesting thing was, as the weekend approached I actually found myself wanting to go. I felt I had a divine appointment, though I wasn't sure what that might mean.

The weekend arrived and I was a stranger at a non-Baptist retreat for the first time in my life. I had no idea what to expect. The only person I knew by name was Rip, but he faithfully took me under his wing and introduced me to several "brothers," including Jack Hollis, the pastor of the church. There was a joyous ease about everyone there, and amongst these Christians I soon settled into a comfortable ease myself. The teaching sessions were rich with life, and my eyes were opened to a new brand of "preaching," a teaching style that was not with a prepared outline, but from a heart that had known and spent time with the Father Himself. The worship surprised me too. I'm not sure now what I thought would happen, but the songs were simple and yet they carried a real message to my heart. A new word was added to my understanding at that retreat: Anointed! There was an anointing that made the presence of Jesus real and near. I don't know if you have experienced what I'm talking about, but that anointing goes beyond talent or vocals or sermons or preachers. It ushers in the very real presence of God Himself. As the weekend went on, I found myself loving this atmosphere and entered into every phase of the retreat, hands raised to heaven, eyes closed, drinking in every drop of His presence.

I won't go into the content or the focus of the teaching, but it opened my eyes to spiritual realities as never before. The time at that retreat was full and rich. I walked into the woods a short distance from everybody else and sat down under a large oak tree. My heart was so very full. I had never experienced the kind of fullness that was now beating within me. I opened my mouth to pray, to thank God for this encounter and suddenly, like a rushing wind, my heart burst, a dam broke. I cried, I laughed, I sang. And then I uttered a word I had never heard before, a word I didn't recognize. Then, another, and another until I was crying, singing, praying in a language I had never learned, spoken or heard. My voice raised in true worship as I sat, stood, and moved around that tree and felt His love flood my soul wave after wave.

I'm not sure how long I stayed there, but when it was over, my soul was renewed, and a mighty work had started. It was a beginning of a new life for me. I realized to my great dismay and release that my problem was that I was an old wine skin, stuck in my old spiritual ways, with no power over sin nor habit, but that now I was being infused with a power that trumped all I had ever experienced or known. And it was real! I hadn't lost my mind, I hadn't gone crazy. I was as clear and alive as life itself. This was not an experience or rite of passage either. This was a taking-up-residence change, darkness-to-light change, lost-but-found change. I didn't know it then, but that retreat would be a turning point in my life, a Jordan crossing, a new way of living, believing, and walking with the Father. I was filled with the Spirit, flooded with His divine power, and washed clean. That weekend, my old wine skin burst and new wine filled me. I was yielded anew and I would never be the same again.

When I returned to the retreat center and saw Bev, she knew instantly what had happened to me. As the retreat ended, we realized something else too. The dark cloud, the heavy spirit that had plagued us, that had caused such consternation for our new marriage, that had stolen our joy, had lifted. Through the years, we have had many ups and downs; many times I have disappointed Beverly, and we've had to work through problems. But the Spirit of God who dispelled the cloud at that retreat has kept us ever since. And that cloud, that cloud has never returned. I've also had some spiritual encounters that have produced only temporary fruit in my life. These have come with a refreshing wind only to dissipate in short order, leaving me much the same as I was before it came. This was not that. My testimony just this: The cloud lifted that day, and I have never been the same since.

The positive ripple effects of my new life with Jesus began almost immediately. The skies were bluer, the trees greener, and the air fresher. All creation seemed new, and I was aware as never before that His power coursed through my life. The heaviness was gone, a new life and a new way of living lay in my future. I was surrendered, no, more than surrendered, I was abandoned to Him.

CHAPTER 8

Unspeakable Joy

For a solid month, I lived under a canopy of His presence such as I'd never known. Every prayer I uttered was almost instantly answered. Every verse I turned to in the Bible seemed alive and written just for me. Every song we sang spoke to me with an intimacy I didn't know existed. The Maranatha Church we unashamedly attended on Tuesday nights brought me such life and fullness. We stayed up long into the night sharing with our new friends and singing the songs of our faith. I stood and testified of the change in my life as soon as I could. I heralded the miraculous change in my life and my marriage, which had survived a kind of "dark night of the soul."

The real change in me was startlingly noticeable right from the start. Not only did I feel different personally, but Bev and I were different as a couple. Suddenly, we loved being together, and our home seemed filled with the Holy Spirit as well. The spirit of heaviness was lifted, and the despair was replaced with an unspeakable joy. Now we were free to love and be loved as never before. We invited folks over, and we prayed and sang and God filled everything and was in everything. We brought the smallest concerns to Him in prayer, and He filled our hearts. This miraculous change was undeniable. His touch on my life broke the chains.

But there was another side effect of this amazing period. Theological study at BBI seemed to distract me from this new-found walk. The students and faculty often spoke of the Charismatic movement that was rapidly moving through the country in the mid to late '70s, and their comments were rarely complimentary. Some laughed at the "antics" they had seen or heard of happening when the "Charismatic's" showed up. Some who were pastoring churches while attending BBI had had "run ins" with "them." Some of these preachers were a little skeptical of anything not Baptist; others were hostile and wanted to keep "those nuts" out of their church.

Not all of my fellow students were aloof and on guard. Several were so passionate about Christ on a personal level and so hungry for a divine move of God in their churches, they relished the fellowship with others so spiritually alive. Russ and Jeannie and Rod and Marie were two such couples. They befriended me from almost the moment I arrived at BBI, and had fully embraced Beverly as soon as they met her. These friends loved God with a passion that dwarfed my own, and they felt called to the Baptist denomination. They were such an encouragement to me as I struggled to gain my bearings, and they provided a source of rich spiritual support and fellowship when I really needed it.

I don't doubt that there were and are many extremes among the Charismatic movement, but the fellowship I had in the Maranatha Church and others of "like precious faith" was balanced and kind in all respects, especially toward those who spoke ill of them. They weren't "weird," and they certainly didn't elevate experience over the scripture. They accepted me as I was, genuinely appreciated my story, and quickly brought me into their family.

On balance, looking back now, the Charismatic movement was more a theological issue than a pragmatic one for the Baptist church, generally, and for BBI and other training centers in the Baptist church ministry, specifically. Unlike Methodists and several other Christian groups, Baptist doctrine did not embrace a separate distinct work of the Holy Spirit. They believed that the Holy Spirit in-fills every believer at the moment of conversion. After conversion, the Spirit works within the believer and leads one to follow the Savior. In addition, the believer could constantly and repeatedly be filled with the Spirit. The emphasis of Baptist theology was that there was not a second work of grace as others maintained, but that there were innumerable works of grace that a believer could and should experience throughout their Christian walk. The real manifestation of salvation and being filled with the Spirit was evidenced by a holy walk. This is what I had believed, enjoyed, and practiced for much of my life. And, for most of my life, I accepted this thinking without debate and had no issues with it.

But when Bev and others began to share their experiences and showed me texts that indicate such a second work as the "Baptism in the Holy Spirit," I found myself studying and praying for a better understanding. Once I had finally experienced that exact "Baptism" personally, those scriptures I had studied and mulled over came alive. I saw this great work of God's grace at the turn of every Bible page. It was not a "strange doctrine" as some had said. It seemed to my mind that it was in fact a central issue and experience of the New Testament believers.

Even now, I still embrace the belief that God wants to work many "in-fillings" of His divine Spirit in the life of the believer over the course of a life lived for Him. There is no question in my mind that the Bible teaches this principle. But in addition to this great truth, I believe there is that "Baptism" that endues believers with a power to be who and what God wants them to be. This is the point where a theological line of demarcation existed between the teaching of BBI and the Baptist denomination, and what I came to believe and experience in my own life. It was not that my experience had taken the place of scriptural truth; it was more that my experience had illuminated scriptural truth.

Three examples might help illustrate what I mean. Mark 8:22-26 describes an event in which Jesus heals a man who was blind. He took the man by the hand, spat on his eyes and laid His hand on him and said, "Do you see anything?" The man responded by saying, "I see *men* like trees, walking around." His blindness was gone but his vision wasn't perfect. Then the Bible says that Jesus again laid His hands on his eyes, looked deep into him, restored him, and that the man could see "everything clearly." I had read the passage many times through the years of my spiritual journey and had never seen it. Jesus, God's son, laid his hand twice on a man who was blind. Immediately the man received some sight. He was no longer in darkness. He could see. We don't know how long he'd been blind, but it isn't hard to believe that the man was ecstatic to have received his sight. His joy must have known no bounds. But things were still unclear. I would draw this as a parallel to me as a believer. My spiritual eyes had been opened at salvation, and I had steadily gained new sight as I walked with the Lord. The Holy Spirit worked in my life bringing truth to me and helping my understanding. But I was still in many ways confused, fearful, and stumbling in an unclear haze. Many nights, lying quietly next to Bev, I'd confess that I had to know all the answers, I was supposed to know all the answers, and it scared me. Nothing she could say would dissuade my fear. It was like "I saw men as trees walking." Then, in the fullness of time for me, Jesus touched me again. A second, distinct, and powerful touch it was, and suddenly I, too, could "see everything clearly." This passage begs the question: Why did Jesus have to lay His hands on the man a second time? Was His power weakened as he had fed the five thousand just before this encounter and therefore He had to touch him twice? Or was there a nugget of truth placed here for those with eyes to see?

As I read I also saw the real change in the disciples with new eyes. Some believe that the disciples were changed from men of fear to men of great faith and power because they had seen the risen Christ. There is no doubt that seeing the Savior alive and strong just days after His brutal crucifixion would have emboldened these men. But the Bible doesn't say that they were emboldened by seeing the risen Lord; it says they waited in Jerusalem and that on the day of Pentecost, the Holy Spirit filled a room where these men were, and they were filled with the Holy Spirit and only then began to preach boldly and perform miracles (Acts 2).

More persuasive still was a passage in Acts, chapter 8. This chapter is rich on many levels and there are enough truths here to camp for a very long time, but in short it says Philip goes to Samaria and preaches to people who were estranged from the Father and in need of His grace. Verse 12 is very poignant. "When (the Samaritans) believed Philip preaching the good news about the kingdom of God and the name of Jesus Christ, they were being baptized." Additionally, the text says, "when Peter and John came down they prayed for them (these believers from Philip's ministry) that they might receive the Holy Spirit." (8:15). The next verse is the clincher: "For He had not fallen upon any of them . . . . and they were receiving the Holy Spirit" (8:16, 17) These scriptures along with many others illustrated to me the scriptural integrity of my new experience.

It's important to remember here that my purpose is to show you the workings of God in my life. My purpose is not to build an air-tight theological argument to convince you of the veracity of my theology nor impress upon you that you should walk in my shoes. While nothing would please me more as a father and grandfather than for my children and grandchildren to walk in His ways, to live their lives in His hands, I here set pen to paper to show the great map of the Father upon which I have charted my course and to let you know that I have loved Him and He has loved me. And that love is your divine heritage too. It was passed to me and I will pass it to you. What you do with it is your choice.

I was learning new things and growing with every passing day. I can't remember a time when I was more alive spiritually than those days. It was almost electric. At the same time, I began to grapple with continuing at BBI. I felt sure that there was no place in the Baptist denomination that would welcome me with open arms. While I still enjoyed some classes, overall I was being drawn away from there. I talked to well-intentioned professors who tried to show me a way to manage my new found passion. I was even passed up the chain of command to the esteemed president of the school. Finally, I told the president that I had been filled with the Holy Spirit and had spoken in tongues. That pretty much closed the conversation. He quickly prayed with me and bid me God's speed, and a moment later, I was no longer a student at BBI.

I in no way intend to put either BBI or the Baptist denomination in an unfavorable light. On the contrary, leaving the Baptist church was incredibly difficult for me. I had been taught the great doctrines of the Bible there, and it was there I had been saved, baptized, and nurtured all my life. It was where my family had grown up, hearing great preaching and teaching. The Baptist church was part of my core, woven in my sinews, wedged into my bones. And these great biblical scholars who taught me were men of God, giants of faith and knowledge. They taught passionately because they were believers and participators in the divine work of God. One could sit at their feet a lifetime and never tire of them sharing the deep truths of scripture. But most excruciating of all, leaving BBI symbolized leaving everything I had ever known. I was new to the Charismatic movement and didn't know anything about how those churches ran or how preachers were called. I knew nothing about networking in this new environ, and many times I wondered if I had made a mistake. I didn't know how I was going to fulfill my call to preach, and once again my future seemed adrift. But there was one thing for sure; I was His, deeper than ever. I had cast off from the shoreline and headed into the deep. My life had changed, and I never seriously considered returning to the old. And from that day to this, I have never looked back.

CHAPTER 9

Embracing the New

In the months since my encounter with God's Holy Spirit, I had grown and learned so much. My appetite for the scripture which had always been acute had become insatiable. I read more and understood more with each passing day. Maranatha Christian Center had aided in my understanding immeasurably. The pastor and leaders of the two hundred or so who assembled each Tuesday night had embraced me as though I had been there for years, and the fellowship was as rich as any I had ever known.

We wanted out of Graceville. Living on "Baptist Row" and so close to BBI was not where we wanted to live. We thought seriously about moving to Marianna since our church fellowship was there, but decided we'd move "home" to enjoy being close to family. As the fall of 1976 drew to a close, Bev and I decided to return to Ocala. Our mobile home would be moved in January with our meager belongings acquired in the first year of marriage: New living room furniture, sofa with matching chair, and a rocker.

Once we were set in Ocala, our top priority was to find a "fellowship" like we had in Marianna. Bev knew many Charismatics, but I was the new kid on the block. We immediately started regularly attending The Word, the Christian coffee house Bev had long been a part of, on Friday nights. No longer uncomfortable in the presence of the moving of the Holy Spirit, I fit right in and met new friends. We searched for a "church" and found that there were two popular fellowships in Ocala. When we went to Christian Fellowship of Ocala, it just seemed to fit. The first Sunday we attended I was "sold." The worship, the informal atmosphere (people would stand up and "testify," sharing fresh stories of what God was doing in their lives), and the spirit of the fellowship made my spirit soar. Bev wasn't as sure as I was, so the next week we went to The Lord's Chapel, a larger group made up of former Baptists who had split away to form a new church. It was well established, and Bev knew many of its participants. While we enjoyed the service (Bev more than I did), I felt that that wasn't the place for us. Our second visit to "The Fellowship" only confirmed to both of us that it was the place we should be. We quickly became regular attendees.

The church quickly became ours. We were there every Sunday and soon became part of every facet of its life. I attended men's meetings and got to know some of the band of brothers who have been my lifelong friends ever since. Bev joined in on the women's group, and before long, we were having fellowships in homes with such lasting friends as John and Terry Curington, Tommy and Diane Wilson, Cliffette and Lamar Holder, and several others. John and I became close friends almost immediately. He stood one day during one of the first services we attended to share something the Lord was showing him, and I knew I wanted to meet him. He was a young contractor and seemed so much more mature than me, but to my surprise and great joy, he became my best friend in a matter of days. He and Terry and Bev and I always found our ways into each other's homes several nights a week. Tom and Donna McIntire, who were instrumental in the teaching ministry at The Word, also became close friends. Tom had a deep understanding of the scripture that I both admired and envied. He had been saved out of the hippie movement, and the spiritual spark in his eyes, and enthusiastic "Praise the Lord" in his greeting made him quite a guy. Though he was far more knowledgeable and experienced than I was, he embraced me as his equal, and we enjoyed informal times together. Many was the time we'd visit in his home, casually talking or playing the card game Hearts. Tommy Wilson played piano at The Fellowship. I had gone through junior and senior high school with him, but only had known him as an acquaintance then. Bev and Cliffette both played guitar and would sing from time to time. Cliffette and Lamar lived on a large farm in Belleview, and Cliffette and Bev quickly became good friends. The Holders had three children, and we spent quite a bit of time on their land, swimming, playing games, and talking about Jesus. In a very short time, we had a family within a family. (I mention these people by name here because these will be familiar to my children, but the entire church body embraced us, and we them.) Once again, I had found a "home."

During the summer of 1977, I received a phone call from a deacon at Wyomina Park Baptist Church, my childhood church that had licensed me to "preach" the year before (the first step to Ordination in the Baptist denomination). Since I was no longer pursuing ordination with the Baptist church, they were withdrawing my license and wanted to arrange to have it returned. Though I understood their position, I was hurt. For me, it was the final breaking away from my ties to being Baptist. What hurt was not that they took away a piece of paper, nor that the door to minister in my home church was being closed. My hurt was that the church that had taught me so much, so well, for so long, the church which had seen me grow and thrive spiritually, was removing their belief that God had called me to the ministry. This was my perception then, not now. I'm older now and understand completely the dilemma the church was in. They could have done nothing else, and what they did, they did with great grace. In fact, this event was a blessing in disguise. I almost immediately saw this as a release, a new freedom to follow God's call wherever it might lead. In a new sense, I was free to follow Papa's will for me. I knew I had a divine call on my life, and while I was not sure how that call was to be realized, it was real. Additionally, it made me search even more fervently to understand and follow God's call on my life. And as it turned out, our fellowship with Wyomina Park as well as many other church denominations has been unhindered and without ill will to any.

During that year we attended Bill Gothard's Institute in Basic Life Principles, the first of many times we attended over several years. This weeklong conference covered everything from sin to parenthood and was so timely for us. I often found myself crying during his sessions, partly because of deep conviction over my many shortcomings and partly because I felt an unusual awareness of God's closeness. As a result, I embarked on a new, more disciplined study of the Bible. He advocated memorizing large passages of scripture and I began that practice with abandon. I memorized Romans, chapter twelve in one night. I also became very aware of my hit-and-miss prayer life at those seminars. I became more intentional in my prayer life. Those two disciplines, serious meditation on the scripture and the development of a more consistent prayer life, made huge differences in my life.

Sometime in mid 1977, Bev and I found out we were going to be parents. We were so excited we could hardly contain our joy. I bought Bev a t-shirt that read "Baby Under Construction" with an arrow pointing to her belly as a way of announcing to our parents and the world that we were going to have a child. We were ecstatic. Joseph Mikel was born in March of 1978. Everyone said a child would change us, that we'd feel a weight of responsibility. In some ways we did, but the truth is that we just took him with us everywhere: home groups, church, friends' houses, and we never missed a beat. We even took him to a Jesus Festival (sort of a Woodstock for Jesus located in Orlando, a three day camping event with music concerts, preaching, and teaching sessions) shortly after he was born.

Toward the end of 1978, we purchased our first real house, complete with three bedrooms, two bathrooms, a formal dining room, and most important, a swimming pool. It seemed so spacious compared to our small mobile home. Joseph's bedroom there had been a glorified closet, but now he had the larger bedroom and his own bathroom (though he wasn't yet potty trained). The larger house made it possible for us to start a home group of our own. John Curington and I were co-leaders, and we averaged about six couples each Sunday night. This was one of my first attempts at any sort of real leadership. John and I were perfect partners, he was relational, I the theologian. He was concerned with how each person was doing; I was concerned with where they were walking with the Lord in the light of His Word. We also began a youth ministry targeted at the middle school age. We had lots of kids come through our house, but several became our core and these have remained friends now through many years: Leah and Kristi Holder, and Graham Barnard and P.J. Wetzel made this ministry both fun and spiritually electric. Though they are all grown now, they provided a wealth of joy and fellowship, and I am blessed by their walk with the Lord to this day. I had no idea at the time that many years hence I would return to this age group to teach full time. We continued to enjoy another home group on Thursday nights too. There, Bev and I would lead singing and share with our good friends. I was learning a new concept, body ministry. Our church had started home groups so that new leaders could be raised up by learning about their gifts in a smaller setting. We loved being used in that setting and for the time, my hunger for "ministry" was satisfied.

It was during this time and the few years after that I finished my Associate of Arts degree in Business at CFCC and attended the University of Florida, majoring in Business. I only spent two semesters at UF and hated every minute of them. I commuted the thirty-five miles each way daily. I struggled with the university's size and impersonal feel. Though I met some Christians on the Plaza, most of the time I felt lost, lonely, and academically over my head. It would be a few more years before God would teach me that I wasn't dumb, a supposition I had held to tightly since seventh grade. When I completed my second semester, I decided not to return for a third.

Late in 1980 I began running. I "caught" the fever from watching Rocky Balboa in the first Rocky movie. My first attempt netted me about a quarter of a mile before I had to start walking. But I kept it up, and before long I was jogging a three mile circuit. I didn't realize it at the time, but that discipline opened a new world of spiritual discipline in my life. The Lord began dealing with my heart about having a more strategic time with Him in prayer and His word. One night, I was in my small study, and I felt God speaking to me. He was saying that I didn't treat him as though He was real.

I questioned Him. "What does that mean?"

He spoke into my heart the truth that I always have time for those that are important in my life. If I had an appointment with someone, I'd be right on time and never miss it. If I overslept or forgot a meeting with my brothers in Christ, I would apologize profusely, begging their forgiveness. Somehow, I didn't treat Papa the same way. I'd plan to get up early and pray, but when I was up later than I had planned, or I just overslept, or awoke too tired, or any number of other things happened, I'd just not show up for that early morning prayer time. I had the idea that He understood, no apology needed! Point of fact was I took Him for granted. And that night He impressed upon me that, though He did understand, the painful truth remained, I valued others more than Him. And then He repeated, "I want you to treat Me like I am real. I Am, you know!"

His words were truth and they pierced my heart. This was one of the first times in my memory that I realized that God was offended by me. I knew that I had offended Him innumerable times, but this idea that the Father "feels" when I neglect Him or replace Him with anything else was brand new to me. I cried at the truth He had so gently placed before me and that night I decided to start a real regimen, both physically and spiritually. I settled into a morning schedule that included writing out my prayers at 5:00 a.m., running three miles and walking one mile at 6:00 a.m., then reading the Bible at 8:00 a.m. That way, I could get it all done before Bev and Joseph woke up. The schedule worked perfectly for years and added a consistency to my spiritual life that had been so lacking. Though I no longer run, I still rise early and spend quiet moments with the Father on a regular basis, searching His word, listening for His voice, longing for His presence, amazing at His grace, embracing His love.

One morning, a few months after I started this devotion time, I overslept. I awoke at 5:15 a.m. and leapt from bed as if awakened by a burglar and ran into the study. The first words I wrote that morning were, "Father, I am so sorry I'm late. I overslept." A gentle peace settled over me as I felt His forgiveness and His forgiveness felt just like a dear friend would have should I arrive late for a meeting with him.

He spoke to me, "Bill, you don't have to do everything perfectly for Me. I just want you to treat me as though I'm real."

Those prayer times and so much more are in three ring notebooks in one of our book cases today. They stand as a testament to my spiritual growth, struggles and triumphs, and the deepening relationship with the Lord I experienced during the early part of the 1980's as I would sit at His feet and learn of Him.

In those quiet morning hours, Father talked to me. He gave me impressions within my spirit, and I grew to feel His gentle wooing in my heart. He taught me during the hour I spent in His word each morning, and I was learning about His interest in my life in ways I'd never known. I systematically read through the Bible, careful to underline verses or phrases that inevitably would jump from the page and into my spirit. I was His child in those moments and His love was tender and real. One morning, as I was in my study reading the Bible, Joseph, then little more than a toddler, came in and crawled up on my lap and sat. He didn't say anything, he didn't want anything, he just sat there in silence and snuggled. At first I was agitated that he was interrupting my quite time with the Lord. But slowly I began to realize that Joseph was doing with me what my heavenly Father had been longing for me to do with Him. He wanted me to sit on His lap, not ask for anything, not say anything, just sit there and let Him snuggle with me. That moment changed the way I have thought about prayer and petitioning the Father. I know He is the One who is eager to answer prayer and has invited us to let our hearts be open to Him. But I learned at the Father's knee that He is so much more than a provider. In fact, most of the things I know about God, the things that really matter, were begun in that tiny room just off the living room during those hours alone with Him. The Bible says, "The anointing which you have received from Him abides (is living) in you, and you have no need for anyone to teach you; But as His anointing teaches you about all things, and is true and is not a lie, and just as it has taught you, you abide in Him" (1 Jn. 2:27). His anointing was teaching me, and I was learning to treat God like He was real. (He is, you know!)

Sometime in the summer of 1982, I felt that the Father was drawing me away for a night of prayer and fasting. Our church was in turmoil, and I had a discomfort, a feeling that a change was coming. I can't explain how that is possible, but I knew that God was up to something in my life. It had begun as a small thought and was now an almost daily ritual, wondering what the Father was up to and what it could mean. Lamar and Cliffette gave me permission to spend the night at the back of their farm. There, they had a comfortable little shack with lawn furniture and a bed, and an old outdoor privy. There was a spring-fed swimming area we had enjoyed through the years, bringing our youth there for fellowships and at other times just enjoying being with Cliffette and Lamar and their amazing family. I packed my sleeping bag, grabbed some water, and made my way for a night alone with God.

I arrived just as the sun was going down. I quickly laid my sleeping bag out, lit the lantern, and found a place beside the water to begin talking to Him. I talked to Him at length about things that were going on at church. I talked about my kids (Christy Marie was born in 1981), and praised Him for where He had brought me. I sang the songs of my faith, and I read random verses from the Bible. Then I sat quietly. I remember humming the chorus, "The greatest thing in all my life is knowing You . . . I want to know You more . . ." Then He spoke to me!

I'm no mystic. I shy away from spiritualizing things too much. I heard no "voice." I saw no vision. I just recognized His voice, speaking in the quiet of my being. I had sat at His feet enough to recognize His voice.

He posed a question to me as out of the clear blue sky: "Would you go back to school if I asked you to?"

The thought caught me off guard. I had quit the University of Florida a few years back and had no intent of returning. I wrestled for a minute with what I had heard, trying to figure it out. Did He want me to go back to school? Or was He merely asking if I was willing to go back to school? I sat quietly and tried to let my thoughts about school (all negative) release, so I could give due process to what the Father was after. I had learned in my quiet time with Him to not jump too fast, but try to stay in step with Him as He worked in my life. I needed that skill that night.

After some time, I gave response to His question. "Father, if YOU are asking me to go back to school, if that is the question, I say yes, but I must know it is what YOU are asking me to do. I have no desire to go back to school. I'm not good at school (at which point I ran through the litany of poor grades and academic struggles dating back to seventh grade). You know this, Father. I have no desire for degrees or titles. But if YOU are asking would I go back to school if YOU asked me to, Father, I say yes, but only for YOU. Not for a degree. Not for a title. Not even for an education. I'm only interested in following You. Only for YOU, yes."

As casually as He had brought up the topic of school, the Father seemed to let it go. I had a sense that He was relaxing back into His chair and pleased that I was willing to do what gave Him pleasure. And soon, my thoughts drifted back, almost in reverse, softly singing, "The greatest thing in all my life is loving You . . . I want to love You more . . ." I praised him and thanked Him for His life in me and for his great grace and goodness in my life. And as I did, I knew that night had served its purpose. I packed my belongings and headed home.

Several weeks passed, and I gave the idea of going to school no thought. It was a simple case of God asking if I was willing, me saying yes, and us resuming our lives. Then one Sunday morning, Elbert Jones' son (Elbert was the pastor/elder of our church) was sharing in the service about going to seminary at Asbury. He was a very engaging speaker, and I enjoyed his sermon, and then promptly moved on, not thinking any more about it.

Then, a few months later, a friend from BBI called me, seemingly out of the blue and asked if I'd come preach for him on a Sunday night. We spoke at length about what had transpired in our lives since my leaving BBI, caught up on each other's family, and a date was agreed upon. We made the trip to Rod Carpenter's home in Smithfield, North Carolina. I don't remember all the particulars of our time with Rod. I do remember taking a jog in the rain and just enjoying their home. They had a quaint older house, and I was particularly fond of the living room. Its high ceilings and casual comfort quickly became my favorite place. In the afternoon, Bev and the Carpenters loaded up the kids and went to a park. I wanted to stay at the house in the cozy living room, and prepare for the evening service.

As I sat in a recliner, I looked around the room, admiring its simple beauty, loving the high stain wooded ceilings. As I was looking up, suddenly I felt His presence. I felt it strongly. It seemed to rush in through the corner of that ceiling, from next to the fireplace top, and powerfully flow down and swirl around me. It was a visible scene; I could see the swirling as in a movie, the wind flying here and yon through the room. It swept over me, it was electric, and I heard Him speak. It was almost audible. The clear words spoken were these: "Asbury . . . Seminary." I heard them over and over. Waves of tears flowed from my eyes as His presence profoundly touched me. A divine electrical current of His Spirit was everywhere present. And I knew that I had been with God, that He had spoken to me, and that He wanted me to go to seminary, not just any seminary, Asbury Seminary. I praised Him. I raised my hands, I shook, I cried, I laughed, I rejoiced. I had heard from God, no doubt, no interpretation or further confirmation was needed. It was a done deal. I could do no other. He had called me to Asbury Seminary, wherever that was. We would soon find out.

In January, 1983, Elbert and his wife Mary and Bev and I made a trip to Asbury in Wilmore, Kentucky. I had applied late in the year and been accepted, and I wanted to see the campus. Wilmore, a very small town and home to both Asbury College and Asbury Theological Seminary, is located about twelve miles outside of Lexington, Kentucky. Horse Country! Beautiful rolling hills! It even snowed while we were there. The college campus looked dreamy: Old brick buildings, a chapel at its center with a pipe organ and grand piano, a clock on the grounds chimed a hymn on the hour. I talked to several professors and listened to others as they taught Old Testament and Greek. I knew this was the place I must go.

I had completed three years of college between my AA degree from Central Florida Community College and course work at the University of Florida and the year at BBI. Asbury College had several requirements to graduate, including two years of a foreign language. I set my course to graduate college in a little over a year, and start Asbury Theological Seminary in the fall of 1984.

God had called me to follow Him at "Asbury . . . Seminary," and it was a lovely place. It was the clearest call I have ever heard, supernatural in its origin, undeniable in its manifestation. I would have to graduate college first, but my course was set. I would leave in the early summer of 1983 and take a full year of Greek in a nine week summer session. Bev would follow in late summer. We would be following Him, and nothing else mattered.

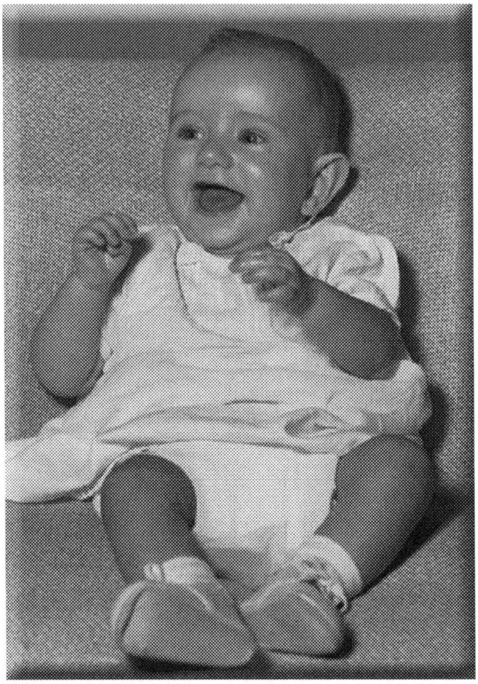
Bill at 6 months – April 1954

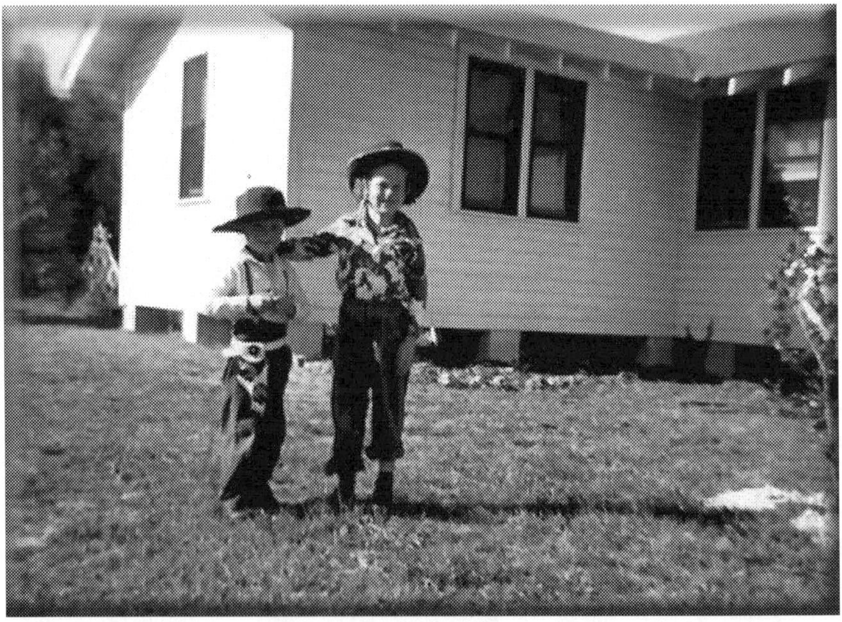
Bill(4 yrs old) & sister Ann in front of their house 1958

Bill's Moms family on her father's side: Front LR- Momma, Granddad Eugene Royal, Grandma Minnie Belle Royal, Minnie Belle. Back Row: Anna Lee, George, Howard, Wesley

Momma Brack's family on her mother's side - The Carrington's

Mom's mom- Minnie Belle Royal

Ann, Bill (about 5 yrs old), Gene

Barney Brack & Mae Royal

Ann, Bill, Gene standing on the front porch before it was enclosed

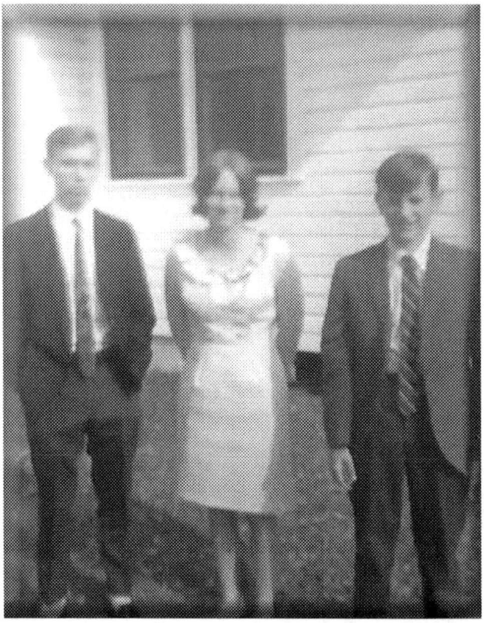

Gene, Ann, Bill (about 13 yrs. old)

Pastor Cooper & Margaret Marshall, Mae & Barney Brack

Aunt Minnie Bell (Mom's sister), Granny Cunningham (who took Dad in when his parents died), Mom & Dad, & Joseph (1982?)

Bill Marine Corp Grad 1971

Our Wedding Day, December 27, 1975

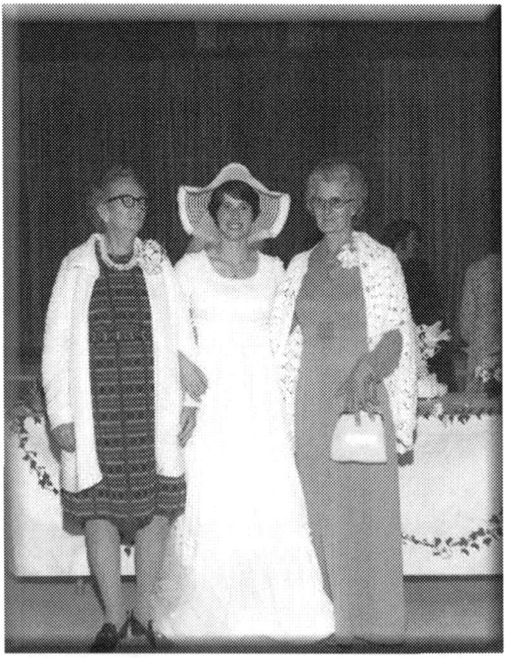

Bev and her grandmothers, Alice Cotton and Daisy Yaxley

Bill, Gene, Ann, taken on our wedding day, December 27, 1975

Bill with his Mom & Dad on Graduation day
from Asbury Seminary (1987)

Joseph, Christy, Philip, John in Kentucky (1986)

The Family right after moving back to Ocala (1987)

The Family (to Iowa then to Bushnell) 1995

Dinner cruise for Bev's 50th birthday- Jan. 16, 1995

Our good friends: Bev, Gail & Bruce Ballard, Terry Curington, Bill, John Curington (Nov 1999)

Our Lifelong friends: Front Row, Ed & Paula Plaster, Terry Curington, Diane & Tommy Wilson. Back Row Bev & Bill, John Curington, Cliffette & Lamar Holder

Our family (2009)

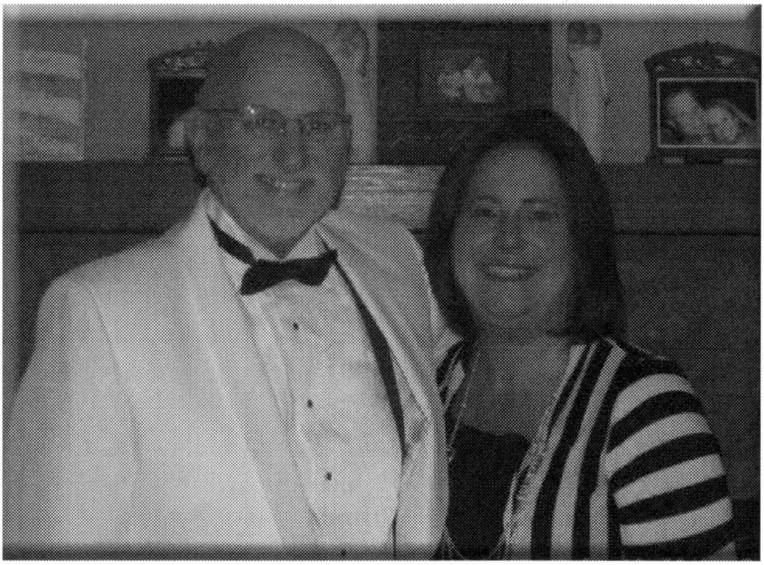
Bill & Bev (2011)

CHAPTER 10

Asbury: Part I

Fully and unreservedly persuaded that God wanted me to go to Asbury, our preparations to move began immediately. His call was clear, but there were many obstacles to overcome and a few hiccups to weather.

One concern was money. Asbury is a private Christian college and seminary, and expensive. I had not even considered the price of the school as I basked in the Father's call, but by the time I would graduate four years later (one year at Asbury College and three years at Asbury Theological Seminary), tuition alone was $190 a credit hour. The Master of Divinity degree I sought was a ninety hour (three year) course of study. I had some GI Bill money left from my military service, but wasn't sure how much. I had no way of knowing how I would pay for four years of college and seminary but as I began the plan to go, I knew money would be tight. I had never borrowed money for school before and with a family that included two small children, it would be quite an undertaking. I knew that with some GI Bill left we could get started, but when I inquired I discovered that I only had a limited amount of time to use it. Back then, a person had ten years to use the GI Bill, a "use it or lose it" sort of policy. I was discharged from the Marines in late 1973, and it was 1983 as we were planning the Asbury move. I applied for and got an extension of benefits, but if I was going to be able to access my military college money, I'd have to do it quickly. This would require me to leave for school several months before I had planned. The upside was that if I started in the summer session, I would have enough college money to make it through my first year of seminary. We decided that I'd go to Kentucky and stay in an efficiency apartment and leave a pregnant Beverly, with Joseph and Christy in Ocala to sell the house and arrange to move later in the summer and in enough time to arrive so Joseph could start first grade on time.

Looking back now, I realize how little I considered how I would pay for school. I don't remember fretting or worrying over it. It wasn't that I was a man of great faith, but I think Bev and I both believed that it would work out somehow and that He would take care of the details. That's been our method of operation for most of our married life. Not that we have been careless or reckless, but through the years we have settled into a comfortable understanding that we are in His hands and that He is more than able to descend to the level of our meager need.

Another obstacle we had to face was selling our house. This would fall on Beverly because I would already be in Kentucky by the time a buyer showed up. The house had been such a blessing in our lives, a provision we had needed even before we knew we'd need it. It had been a place of both family get-togethers and ministry. It was also the place where I had learned deep lessons at the Father's knee, many of which are still working in my life as I write now. But we could ill afford two house payments, and as we made plans to move, selling the house was an imperative. We set about making it as appealing to prospective buyers as possible. Like many, we made the repairs we had long been putting off so we could relinquish ownership and chase after Papa.

Not long after I began school at Asbury, Bev called with the news about a buyer. They wanted to buy the house, but wanted to make an annual payment for five years with a balloon payment at the end of that time. With no other offers, we sold the house on those terms. Father was active in this as we found out. Each year the thousand dollars came in and each year, it met specific needs. And it reminded us on an annual basis that He was there to meet our needs.

A third concern was our home church. We had been through some rough changes including a split over conflicts within leadership, and we had left with many others. By the time God called us to Asbury, Bev and I were worship and youth group leaders of the new church. Elbert Jones had added me to his staff, and we met regularly to pray and plan. Though he was in wholehearted agreement that God had indeed called me to Asbury, I felt that I was leaving him at an important time. Part of me wanted to stay through the summer and begin school in the fall term, but I couldn't with GI Bill being what it was. But there was another part of me that was relieved to be leaving those hard months behind. Even so, we were tugged by the love of that little fellowship, and leaving wasn't as easy as I thought it would be. Through the years I have often gone back to the days at the Fellowship and found great solace, remembering what I learned and how I grew there.

Finally, there was the emotional dimension of leaving family and friends. I was so focused on Asbury and following the Father, I paid little attention to what we were leaving behind. But Bev felt it acutely and would struggle, not with His call, but with the emotions of being taken from her dearest friends. When the church split, some of my dearest friends stayed with the other church; consequently, Bev's relationships ran deeper than mine did at that time, and amongst the many things we had to do to be ready to move, we prepared to say goodbyes to people who really mattered. To my embarrassment, I confess that I was oblivious of Bev's fears and feelings, and just pressed forward with my vision and His calling.

We had traded our 1977 Dodge Van in on a Volkswagen rabbit that got 50 miles per gallon. We thought that was an excellent idea to save money on traveling back and forth from Kentucky to Florida. Joseph was five and Christy was one, and they'd fit perfectly in our new little car. Or so we thought. In the midst of our planning and overcoming all obstacles to following the call to Asbury, we discovered that Bev was pregnant with Philip. While we were both shocked and wondered about the timing, we embraced the idea of three kids, taking it in stride with a "what's one more" attitude.

When the time came for me to leave, I said my goodbyes, loaded up the Rabbit, bike hanging off the back, and excitedly took off. I was so glad to be on my way after months of planning and the whirlwind of activities that accompanied it. I had reserved a one room efficiency to live in within walking distance of the college and was ready to enroll in my first course, Greek. I stopped in Atlanta to spend the night with Brother and Mrs. Marshall, an ironic circle from my distant youth. As always, they were supportive, proud of me, and enthusiastic to learn that I was finally following God's call. I knew what they meant, but I also realized that I had been doing that all along, just trying to figure out what that was.

I arrived and settled in my room, met a few others attending the summer term. I went to registration and discovered that beards were not allowed in school and had to shave mine before the following day's class, a fact not mentioned during my visit earlier in the year. I went to the school bookstore, purchased my supplies, and steadied myself for a summer away from my family, and the ominous task of learning to read and understand Greek.

Classes were held at eight o'clock in the morning and lasted until eleven-thirty. We had a daily vocabulary test with about twenty-five words, along with some translation to be ready for each day. After classes, I'd study from one o'clock until five. Then, I'd run my three miles, and hit the books again from seven until the library closed at ten. Every Friday was a unit test. The schedule was brutal, and I was glad that I had no other distractions. Every waking minute was consumed with thoughts of learning this language that had been used to pen the great majority of the New Testament.

The class was small, only five students crazy enough to try to press a year of Greek into just nine weeks. We formed a group and studied together; quizzed each other, and fellowshipped. Soon, I met others on campus taking classes in Hebrew, history, and a variety of other subjects, several of whom became great friends. God lavished me with these immediate friends who helped quell my loneliness and deflected my fears.

One day, the first week of classes, the professor was explaining a concept. I was lost. I had no idea what he was trying to get across. I had felt that kind of panicked emotion many times going all the way back to junior high school. Before, I had always assumed that I was just too dumb to understand, but this was different. I was at this college, at this time, following Father's call, and I couldn't just sit and stare as before. There was nowhere to hide, only four others and me. With much trembling, I raised my hand and asked a question, something I can't remember ever doing. I was afraid of appearing stupid, but I had a greater fear. I feared that I would fail, that I would let the Father who had so lovingly and surely called me there, down, that all my plans and leaving my family would end in my "did not finish" status. So, I raised my hand. I asked whatever question I had (something about the Greek equivalent to the English indirect object). The patient professor, as if he saw my shy timidity, gently and clearly explained the concept so that even a simpleton such as I could understand. When he finished, down the row to my left, Keith Boone exclaimed, "Oh!"

In that moment I had an epiphany. I was not the only one sitting in that classroom who did not understand that simple concept. My mind raced with wondering how many people I had failed to help understand things simply because I was too scared to raise my hand and ask my questions. This opened a whole new world to me, and I became the class questioner. Every day, my hand went up. I even offered answers to others questions. Sometimes I was incorrect, sometimes correct, but I broke a lifetime barrier. I felt exhilarated, and the more I asked and participated, the more I understood. That day was the start of a new academic day for me. The results were almost immediate. My grades soared, my understanding expanded, and I began to feel something I never had in academia, confidence. The Father knew I would need that in the weeks and years ahead, and He had provided that small classroom with a very patient teacher to give me a safe place to practice asking questions. From that day onward, I asked questions, got both answers and good grades.

I also busied myself with finding a good church for our family. Some of my new friends suggested First Assembly of God in Lexington, twelve miles away. I had no intention of becoming part of a denominational church, but on my first visit, I fell in love with Pastor Ken Groen. His gentle style and practical preaching were a winning combination and that's where we attended the entirety of our time in Kentucky. By the time Bev and the kids arrived, I felt at home there, had made some friends, and was more than anxious to attend church together as a family again.

Meanwhile, Bev was working tirelessly to get the house ready for sale and making arrangements to move. With two small children and one "in the oven" she plodded on through the dog days of the summer of 1983. In addition, she continued to work in her dad's rubber stamp shop, lead worship at church, and a myriad of other things that made it possible for me to concentrate on my studies.

I'll talk more about the blessing that Bev has been to me later, but it must be said here that there would have been no way that I could have run after the Father's call without the life partner He had given me. At our wedding, she had sung the song "Let Us Climb the Hill Together." She has "climbed" with me for each of our years together (thirty-seven as of this writing), but never more than in the days leading up to her move to Asbury. She had bought into God's call and never looked back. She never second guessed, argued about, resisted because, nor complained over . . . she just loved me and the Father, and was all in. No backup plan, no regrets, she was and still is one of a kind. She is a rare diamond who I was fortunate to find, and she has been priceless to me for each of these many years. Early in our relationship, I wrote her a message that God gave me about her. I quoted it to her on our wedding day. It reads in part, "Do you dare not love that which I have given you? She will become to you more precious than gold . . ." And He was so right; she has been just that, priceless!

In mid July, Bev and the kids made the move to Kentucky. I found a nice house in a small town five miles from Asbury (there were no houses available in the Wilmore community where Asbury is located). Our dear friends Lamar and Cliffette Holder came with her, Lamar driving the seven hundred fifty miles in a giant U-Haul without air conditioning. When they arrived, they were greeted by one of the hottest summers Kentucky had on record. They helped us unload and get reasonably settled before they returned home.

Though the house was nice with three bedrooms and a full basement, it had one fatal flaw. It was not air conditioned. As the temperatures climbed into the high 90s with humidity near the same, and then stayed there days on end, Bev and the kids sweltered as they tried to get unpacked and set up housekeeping. I took the VW Rabbit to school each day, stayed there to study in the air conditioned campus library, and then would head home about five in the afternoon in the air conditioned car. Needless to say, it didn't take me many days coming in all chipper and looking at my haggard tribe to know that we would have to find the money to buy a large window unit. This we did almost immediately and the atmosphere in our home took a notable upturn.

Before I finished that summer school session, we received a letter from our home church in Ocala. Its contents surprised, no, startled us to the core. Our little church of less than one hundred people at the time of our leaving; the members were mostly families with small children like us, very few folks of great wealth, yet that church had committed to pay the entire cost of my first year at Asbury. We were humbled and amazed that we were even in their thoughts at that moment, and knew that God was confirming to us His call through them. Every month we got a check from the church that we set aside to pay for school. That little church buoyed our spirits and made it possible to pay three of the four years at Asbury without debt of any kind, and live comfortably. Even though we never returned to the church permanently, we'll never forget their generosity and love showed to us. God was meeting our needs through them as we took one step at a time with Him.

I finished Asbury College in the summer of 1984, having completed a degree in business with two years of Greek and with only one "B", all other grades were "A's." I had learned so much about myself. I discovered that I was smart, that I could understand difficult concepts, that I could make good grades, and that I could succeed. I had made friends and had initiated a prayer meeting with a small group of guys and was building relationships. Our son Philip had been born and I was looking forward to seminary, the real reason I had come to Asbury in the first place. God had called me to "Asbury . . . Seminary" and everything I had done so far was so that I could go there. Asbury Theological Seminary was just across the street from the college, but it was a thousand miles in terms of my future.

CHAPTER 11

Asbury: Part II

Lexington Avenue separated the college campus from the seminary. It was the main drag through town and if you headed south it would dead end in at a place called High Bridge. I'd often run that way on my seven and one half mile loop in the countryside. Taking Lexington Avenue north ended in Lexington, Kentucky, the place where we shopped and went to church. That avenue was the Jordan River of my education, my calling, and I was thrilled when September 1984 rolled around and I was in "Asbury . . . Seminary."

The seminary consisted of people from many places in the United States and other countries as well. They came from many walks of life, and many life experiences. Some were single, others had large families. Some were poor, some were affluent. We were from many denominations and schools of thought, but all were there because we felt the divine tug of God on our hearts and lives.

One of the very first courses in seminary was Christian Theology, a core requirement for everyone. Our first test would set the pace for us as we tried to conquer the myriad of tasks that would make up seminary curricula. As the tests were returned, the professor called out my name. "Who is Bill Brack?"

I reluctantly raised my hand. A shiver ran through me as I remembered academic failures from my junior high school days. I had studied long and hard for this theology test, over fifteen hours.

"Bill Brack scored the highest grade in the class."

I was the top contender of the sixty students, and was awarded a ninety eight for my efforts. When class ended that day, I had a number of students congratulate me. Among them were five guys who came to me as a group to invite me to become study buddies with them. This group consisted of an executive from AT&T, a pharmacist, a lawyer, a Biblical Languages major, and my good friend from college who was fluent in Hebrew studies. All of them were truly smart and they wanted me to join them! They became my steady study friends throughout my seminary days. A scripture verse I had memorized came to my mind, "He who walks with wise men will be wise" (Proverbs 13:20). Much of my steady success in seminary is attributed squarely on those "wise men" with whom I was able to associate and study.

Later I had the opportunity to take The Book of Revelation, a course with Dr. Mullhulland, a noted scholar who had written a unique manuscript for his book, *The Revelation: New Jerusalem Living in a Fallen Babylon World,* while he was on sabbatical. This particular class was, for me, the most meaningful class I took in all of seminary. I had no real understanding of the Revelation and had only grasped the book's meaning in a cursory way. But that course opened my eyes to the great teachings of this wonderful book. I discovered Dr. Mullhulland's approach to be the most practical explanation I had ever encountered and clarified some of the great ambiguities of interpretations of this last book of the Bible. Since that class, I have had the opportunity to teach the book of Revelation many times and have discovered fresh insights and applications every time. An added bonus of the class was that I had the chance to translate the entire Revelation from Greek to English. It helped hone my Greek skills and gave me greater competence and confidence when translating other New Testament books and texts that I have used throughout my life.

That is not to say that other classes were insignificant to the formation of my thoughts and life from those seminary days. From inductive Bible study to spiritual formation classes, from language studies to missions, from philosophy to church history, and everything between, I found such a wealth of information, that to overlook any would do disservice to them all. Each class and each professor taught from not only a rich educational depth, but also from a spirit of love of the Father, His people, and His mission. That love was contagious. I wanted to be the kind of person I witnessed in each of them; a head, sharp with truth, and a heart "strangely warmed."

In addition to course study, the seminary required three courses in practical ministry; one in a secular institution, and two in a church ministry context. These were designed to take us out of the world of strict academia and into the "real" world of ministry. I had the opportunity to be an assistant chaplain in the Veterans Administration Hospital in Lexington. When no one was eager to step forward to volunteer for the "Psych Ward," I reluctantly did. I felt that I was an obvious choice since I had been in the military, and our Presbyterian chaplain assigned me with enthusiasm. What I encountered there was certainly beyond my training and beyond anything I had ever seen. Though I understood the concept of Post Traumatic Stress Syndrome and had mildly tasted it as I struggled with my own military trials, I had never faced demons as dark and menacing as those who had been placed into psychiatric care. They shared their stories with me, the nightmarish dreams that plagued them, and the events that had transformed them from invincible soldiers to almost vegetables. I appreciated their sacrifices and gained a new understanding of the need for grace in all our lives. Though it paled in comparison, I shared some of my own story, and found these patients eager to embrace me as their brother and show me the grace of God. I was unable to "cure" them, and I couldn't take their fears or dreams away, but I did take with me an unending compassion for those struggle. (Since that experience, I have often shared the funny situations I encountered there. But I have never divulged the deep fears that these brave warriors shared with me. Many times they opened up to me with the cautious disclaimer, "I've never told anyone this. Promise me not to repeat this." I so deeply related to that request, I have kept their secrets as I have mine, in some cases more so.)

The Psych Ward was not my only assignment at the V.A. Hospital. Each of the five of us in the V.A. group were tasked with helping visit all the patients, praying if they requested, and inviting each to come to the chapel services. We would go to each room with a bulletin and share both the Protestant and Catholic service times. We were allowed to participate in the services by leading singing or prayer and reading the scripture passages. In some cases we were allowed to bring the homily (message) for the service. I found that I related well to all denominations and was struck by how broad the term "Christian" applies. To my great surprise, I discovered that even Catholics might be Christian. (I say this now tongue in cheek and understand the absurdity of such a statement. From time to time over the years I have wondered if some Pentecostals and Baptists were Christians, too.) Though I have never adopted their theology as my own, I gained an appreciation for their work and ministry to those who were suffering. Once I was even summoned to a death bed to administer "last rites" when the Catholic priest was unable to come. That practical ministry foreshadowed what was to become my favorite part of pastoral work later on, hospital and shut-in visitation.

I approached Pastor Groen at First Assembly, the church we attended the entire time we were at Asbury, and asked if I could do my practicum ministry with him. He was a graduate of Asbury Seminary himself and embraced all the students who attended the church and eagerly approved my involvement there. Pastor Steve Gehring, the educational pastor at the church would be my supervisor for my two semesters of ministry. We met and decided that my ministry would concentrate on developing a Sunday school class for young married couples to help fill a gap. My job was to integrate and assimilate new couples into the life of the church. I would be tasked with developing the class itself and would help the church staff by contacting visiting families at the church. I partnered with another seminarian to host the new class. The class clicked almost immediately, and we forged great new friendships. It had "scratched an itch," and soon the class had about ten couples who attended regularly. In addition to the actual class, where coffee, juice, and snacks were shared, the group also met in homes for fellowship or a Saturday outing. In this way, we saw several families about our age not only become committed members of First Assembly, but our good friends as well.

Martin Jacobsen, the youth pastor there, and I became quick friends. He was leaving to go to the mission field soon, but we enjoyed a great and rich friendship with him and his wife Charlotte and their two children. Our little Sunday school class hosted a mission's dinner to raise money for them. I also had the opportunity to go with Martin several times as he traveled the state to raise the funds he would need to go to language school and then on to Argentina.

In 1985, I had an opportunity to go on a mission's trip to Costa Rica with my brother Gene's church in Hattiesburg, Mississippi. I broached the subject with Pastor Groen, and he committed one hundred of the needed seven hundred and fifty dollars. He helped me form a letter asking for friends to support me. The money came in just as he said it would, and that summer I left the country for the first time since my military days.

While there, I was able to lead a team into the deep Costa Rican jungles to preach and fellowship with churches there. We traveled by bus, then car, and finally on foot. The churches were primitive by American standards, some with a candle dangling from the rafters, the pulpit hammered into the hard dirt floor. Every service was packed with people, some of whom had walked four miles just to attend. I've never felt so inadequate and humbled in my life. What could I tell these folks about Christ that they didn't already know and experience in their own lives on a daily basis? Certainly, their commitments were deeper than mine, and yet God used me and the team in powerful ways.

When we returned to San Jose for a few last services, I saw a miracle unlike any I had ever experienced before or since. After the preaching was over and we were praying with people, an elderly lady approached me for prayer. I prayed for her as best I could in English, and then in tongues. As I prayed, she swayed as under an anointing from God, and she began to sing. It was hard to hear her because the place was rather noisy, as Pentecostal services can often be, so I moved closer to hear her better. She sang with a beautiful soprano voice. I leaned closer and heard her clear praises rise to God . . . "in English". I questioned those around us and they told me she could not speak English and that I was hearing a woman singing to God in a language she had never learned. Remembering it now brings back goose bumps and the thrill of that moment. It not only excited me then, but has remained a moment frozen in time when God showed me His reality again.

Back in Kentucky, Pastor Groen also asked if I would lead the worship in the early Sunday morning service and often the evening as well. Bev and I did this enthusiastically and were spiritually stretched by the experience. We became card-carrying members of the church and I began to pursue ministerial ordination credentials with the Assemblies of God denomination.

While most of my seminary costs were paid through the G.I. bill and the faithful support of our small church in Ocala, money was always short. John Mark was born during the middle of my second year in seminary, and now we had four children who traveled with us in our ever shrinking Volkswagen Rabbit. Even though money was tight, we were able to go to McDonalds' for breakfast almost every week. We visited places close by and enjoyed the mountains not far away, camping and sightseeing.

As my final year of seminary approached, school money was gone. I had to borrow five thousand dollars to finish seminary, a widow's mite now, but then, a monumental amount. Along the way, we had seen God provide for us in miraculous and natural and supernatural ways. Bev's mom would come to visit and buy the kids school clothes each year. An unexpected check arrived one day for over six thousand dollars. This enabled us to buy a Safari minivan, a vehicle that seemed a mansion after being jammed together in the VW Rabbit all those years. One night we came home from Sunday night church to discover our front porch covered with bags of groceries. An estimated five hundred dollars worth of food, toiletries, and goodies provided for our needs for quite some time. Those are just some examples of God's provision to us in our seminary years.

Even with a loan for school, I discovered that I still owed money to the school as graduation approached. I prayed that God would provide the needed money. I busied myself with the class schedule and remember those last two semesters as the hardest of all. I had twenty one papers or projects, several of them over twenty pages in length. But as graduation day neared, no money was coming in. I learned that unless my bill was paid in full, I could walk but would not receive my diploma. The thought dismayed and worried me. I began to beg God to provide. That piece of paper was my coronation and I wanted it badly. God had called me to Asbury Seminary, and I knew somehow that He would provide. I filled my mind with His faithfulness in the past and struggled to trust him for this small amount to allow me to finish, degree in hand. I checked the accounting office almost daily as the big day approached and each day was disappointed that no money had miraculously appeared in my school account. Nevertheless, I believed that He would bring in the needed funds somehow. The day before graduation, I again checked with the accounting office. No money. But I trusted deeply that Father would come to my rescue and that my diploma would be in the impressive Asbury Theological Seminary jacket. On graduation day, while my parents and sister, Bev and my four children looked on, I walked across the platform, shook hands with the president of the seminary and received the closed diploma jacket and returned to my seat. I sat nervously a moment, prayed one last prayer and opened the jacket. Inside? Nothing!

It seems almost trivial now, the Father's healing is so complete, but in that moment and for years to come, I carried a disappointment with God so deep I can't adequately describe it. I had followed His lead; going to seminary was His idea, not mine, and though He had faithfully walked with me through every trial, I was hurt deep in my spirit that He had let me down at this last moment. I felt I had done all He had asked of me and He had failed to come through.

During my seminary experiences, a subtle but fatal shift had slowly occurred in my thinking. I had begun to buy into the idea that He had called me to ministry—that I was there for the purpose of preparing for something He wanted me to "do." I thought I was supposed to leave seminary with a degree that made me marketable to a church so I could be hired as a pastor or staff member of a church. I was actively pursuing credentials for that purpose. But my fatal assumption was that He had called me to "do" something. In reality, He had called me to Himself, to learn of Him. The degree, the place of ministry, the frills of denominational and pastoral offices was not on His mind. It would take me years to understand that, and in the meantime, I carried a deep disappointment with Him at not providing a small amount of money to pay for a piece of paper, a piece of paper about which, for me, He couldn't have cared less. I would leave seminary with a first class education, rich spiritual and relational experiences, two additional children, a five thousand dollar school loan, an uncertainty of the future, and a ripping disappointment with the Author and Perfecter of my faith. With no denominational appointment and not enough money to stay living in Kentucky, we moved back to Ocala to seek a pastoral position somewhere close to family in Florida. Even to write the words "seek a pastoral position" grieves me now, but at that time, that was my mentality, and no admiration or admonition could make me see otherwise. Surely, a seminary degree meant a professional ministry position, and a professional position would make me complete. How wrong I was.

CHAPTER 12

The Ministry . . . Going Full Time

Our good friends John and Terry Curington (lifelong friends from our Christian Fellowship days) drove a U-haul truck to Wilmore, Kentucky to help us move back to Ocala. It was actually cheaper than renting a truck from Lexington. Friends from First Assembly in Lexington came and helped load the biggest truck U-haul had. We rented a small three bedroom house on the southeast side of Ocala which would be our base camp as I looked for a ministry position. It was the summer of 1987.

Soon after we arrived, we picked up where we had left off. We worked in Bev's dad's rubber stamp business, and I sent out resumes. In short order, I made an appointment with Pastor Fred McDaniel, senior pastor of First Assembly of God in Ocala, a large church of about thousand members. It had grown fast after some of the debacles of the Charismatic churches in town, and we knew several people there from days gone by. Pastor McDaniel led me into his comfortable office and I shared my call to ministry, about Asbury, and made myself available for anything I could do to help him as I looked for a position in a church somewhere. I discovered that he was Assistant Presbyter of the Ocala section of the Assemblies of God, and that he had connections all over Florida, a gold mine in terms of the possibilities he could open for me. Beyond that, he was friendly and we hit it off almost immediately.

We quickly settled into attending that church, the kids in Missionettes and Royal Rangers, and Bev and I into Sunday school. Larry Noel was the children's pastor and an energetic and outgoing person who loved what he did and was quite good at it. Ron Hyatt was the youth pastor, and Joseph was soon taking part in his activities. Tim Davis, the minister of music, was an amazing singer, and pianist. The church had a prayer meeting on Thursday mornings at six, and I began to attend those regularly. Slowly at first, but soon in retrospect, Pastor McDaniel and I developed a friendship. He would sometimes ask if I would go visit people with him, and so we'd go to hospitals or nursing homes, or wherever he needed to go, often stopping at car lots to look around, something we both enjoyed. Some of those visits took us to Gainesville where we would visit, have lunch, and talk.

Through the process of time, Pastor McDaniel wanted me to do a seminar for the Sunday school and children's departments about reaching and assimilating new people for the church. I put together a packet, and on a Thursday night, I presented it to a group of about thirty church workers. The point was to have these leaders look beyond teaching a lesson, and to become caregivers to the people who were part of their ministry. The seminar was well received, and I felt a sense of fulfillment as I left the church that night.

I began doing visitation on Tuesdays soon after the seminar, spending almost all day searching for homes and visiting newcomers to First Assembly. After several weeks of visiting newcomers to the church, I wrote a report for the board to consider as the church grew. I mentioned my two findings. One was that many were surprised and pleased that someone from a church the size of First Assembly would actually knock on their doors to welcome them, thank them for their visit to the church, and offer help in getting them involved. I was a go-between guy that linked a larger church to the more important smaller connections they needed. The other finding was that many of these new attendees were single. I recommended in my report that as the church looked to the future, they should consider a staff position that would be responsible for expanding a ministry to new-comers and that an official ministry should be added for singles.

Over the next few months, Pastor McDaniel and I visited quite frequently and soon began talking about having me come on staff as a visitation pastor. Our personalities seemed to match, and we both agreed on many of the issues facing the Church at the time. We grappled with theology and practice policies, and I found that we saw eye to eye on most key issues. I became excited at the possibility of joining the ministerial staff with him. We worked out the logistics and details, and around October,

I was officially placed on staff, given an office, a title, and business cards. I had arrived!

I immediately began to immerse myself in the work I had been assigned. I set myself the schedule of visiting the people who had filled out visitation cards in the Sunday services. I learned how to get around the growing Ocala area and spent every Tuesday for the next four and a half years on the road. In addition, I was assigned the development of a singles ministry, about which I knew almost nothing. I was placed on the platform as an associate pastor and became the bumbling announcement maker. Little did I know that my nervousness and mistakes at making announcements made me appear 'real' and approachable to the crowds who attended the church. Suddenly, people wanted to talk with me, seeking my counsel on anything from family problems to helping them through the grief process after a death. I enjoyed attending staff meetings and being part of the workings of the church. I traveled to both sectional and district meetings, and in two years, I was ordained as an Assemblies of God minister. I was asked to be present at every board meeting, and for the first time saw that not everyone involved in the church loved the pastor as I had assumed when observing my own deacon father during my growing up years. My father never uttered a breath of criticism for any pastor our church ever had. On this board, things were different. In fact, some, though only a small minority, wanted the pastor to leave, an unsettling taste of reality that would sting me through the years. The ministerial staff on the other hand, attended every funeral along with Pastor McDaniel and had a great relationship. It was fun to be part of such a grand commodore.

Along the way, we had a promotion for the annual Sunday School convention. The theme was "Vote for Sunday School." Our staff, minus Pastor McDaniel, formed a quartet to sing the promotional theme song. The church went crazy as we sang, all four parts of the quartet harmony present in the four members of the pastoral staff. The church wanted more, so Tim formed us into a quartet called "The Pastors' Four." Over the years we would sing from time to time, and each time, we received an overwhelmingly positive response. Once we even had a Missions benefit concert on a Sunday night, raising thousands of dollars for a ministry trip to Venezuela. Later, Pastor asked me to accompany him to Venezuela on a fact finding mission, scouting out places to stay, arranging accommodations, and meeting the missionary contact there. On the flight home, Pastor asked me to lead the twenty-four man team who would put a second floor on a bible school there, an assignment I willingly accepted. The church produced some grand seasonal presentations; the grandest of them all was the Christmas musical, "The Gospel According to Scrooge." I was cast in the musical every year I was there and enjoyed acting for the first time. I made friends with other ministers throughout our section and the district, and I felt that I had found a home.

I say all that to give you a feel for what I did at First Assembly and to show that I was enjoying being in vocational full-time ministry for the first time in my life. I was busy, fulfilled, and involved. But I was so engrossed in what I was doing and the busyness of it, I didn't even recognize that Bev was dying, not physically, but spiritually. She felt a certain "disconnect" from the other pastors' wives at the time, and though she was always supportive and engaged in the ministry, she felt an uneasiness with what she thought was a "show." That is not to say she was judgmental or aloof or uninvolved. She was a faithful member of the church, an amazing support for me, and an involved participant in the life of the church. She would go visiting with me from time to time and attended every function dutifully and faithfully. She was an amazing supporter of the singles ministry we started and watched with me the growth of a core group of around thirty with some outings that gathered as many as seventy people.

I say that I didn't recognize Bev's feelings, but my blindness was more than a total lack of awareness or recognition. The truth is I was oblivious. I thought she was sometimes awkward about things because she didn't know the people in my new world as well as I and that if she just spent more time with them she'd see what I saw and be fine. Looking back now, my lack of sensitivity grieves me. But I was so caught up in what I was doing, I honestly didn't see. I share this as a warning for anyone who might happen upon these pages. Watch out for the many pitfalls that "professional ministry" can hold.

Equally disconcerting was a blindness that slowly began to engulf me, the blindness of how far I had strayed from the days when I enjoyed a fresh and vibrant relationship with Jesus, forged through delightful hours reading His word and in fellowship at His knee in prayer. My prayer life now consisted largely of praying before and after a meeting, or praying during the Thursday morning prayer hour, or praying for the sick in the hospital or while on visitation. My devotional reading of the scriptures that had formed my heart after Him was replaced with the pressure of preparing to preach or lead Bible study classes.

The slope that leads to active involvement in ministry can be slippery. Mine started as soon as I began studies at Asbury. My time alone with the Father had steadily shrunk as I spent more and more time learning the Bible, studying languages so I could better understand and then present Bible truth to others, and indulging myself in the addiction of good grades. Then, at First Assembly and afterwards, I was so busy with doing the work of God, I sacrificed my devotional time on the altar of service for Him and His church. It is possible to do this for a while, but it is only a matter of time until it takes its toll and the spiritual fuel runs out. For me, it would be years before I would regain the balance that all Christians must strike. No matter their career or ministry involvement, there must be a balance of "being" with the pressures of "doing." Of course, I can only see this after the fact, but wise is the man or woman who can quickly discern and quickly turn away from this particular pitfall and make the adjustments required to "return to their first love." I had bought an enticing bag of goods and was enjoying them completely, not truly realizing or being appalled that I was losing touch with "my own first love," my connection to the Father. And in the absence of that connection, not only is ministry affected, but far more important, the life blood that first produced its fire dies. I ignored the death rattle, surmising I needed a vacation or seminar, or some ministerial retreat. This was the "uncomfortable" feeling Bev had. I didn't know it then, but in addition to Bev's death throes, my own death at the hands of ministry had already begun.

CHAPTER 13

To Iowa and Back

Unaware that a dying process had already begun in my spiritual life, I loved being in Ocala and was content for a while, but after about three years I started experiencing a restlessness in my heart. About this same time, Bev remembers an evening service where we were both at the altar praying, separately, and God simultaneously planted a Word in both our hearts, "to be ready, change is coming." Though I loved First Assembly, this word spoken to Bev and I caused me to be open to the possibility of something different.

Early in 1990, Ron Hyatt, the youth pastor, left First Assembly to take a pastorate in Mississippi. His leaving started me thinking about my future in ministry too, but only in a cursory way. I was content at First Assembly and comfortable. But with his leaving, I gradually became more restless myself and wanted, not so much to move to a new town, as to move into different ministries and away from the grind of visitation and singles. I wasn't unhappy per se, and I wasn't sure what I really wanted, but I felt that I was in a rut. I didn't want to leave Ocala, but I did want a new start. In retrospect, feelings of restlessness and discontent have often been God's way of bringing me to both a willingness to follow Him and an excitement that comes with following Him in a dynamic relationship where change opens new doors.

As time passed, my restlessness became more pronounced. Early in 1992, Ron Hyatt transferred to take a pastorate in Davenport, Iowa, and called me to see if I was interested in being his Associate Pastor in charge of Christian Education and Pastoral Care. I flew to Iowa to see the church and talk to Ron. The church was smaller than First Assembly, but had a great facility and was known for bringing in the lost through a vibrant bus ministry. Ron had a vision for growing the church, and remembering that we had worked well together in Ocala, I committed to joining him there. It seemed like an answer for my restlessness at First Assembly and would give me the new start I had been seeking. When I returned from Iowa, I told Pastor McDaniel that I would be leaving in June. I'm not sure, but I think he was disappointed that I would leave First Assembly to go work with Ron. Nonetheless, I began to make preparations to move.

In May, I led the mission's team to Venezuela to continue work on a Bible school there. I remember it as an uneventful trip. When we returned from Venezuela, I gave my formal announcement to the congregation stating that I was leaving for Iowa. To my surprise, many shocked parishioners cried and asked me to please stay. But the decision had been made, and in mid-June, a truck with all our household goods was loaded, and we set off for Davenport, Iowa and what we believed was God's new adventure for us.

Westside Assembly of God opened its doors wide for us. But from the day we arrived, things began to fall apart. Ron had told us prior to our departure that he was looking for a house for us, but when we got there, no house had been found. We spent four days in a motel, which the kids loved because of the indoor swimming pool and pool table, as Bev and I frantically looked for a house. A man Ron had talked to about the position I took quickly befriended us and helped us find suitable temporary housing, an old two-story home in a questionable neighborhood. We lived there only one month and then moved to a house outside of town. This new home, though small for six people, was located in a picturesque neighborhood called Parkview. A park ran in back of our house and intertwined throughout the neighborhood. Just a short distance away was a county park where deer grazed and families picnicked, and our small Yorkie, Rimshot, frolicked, chasing deer and running himself exhausted. Our family spent lots of wonderful times at Scott County Park.

I began working almost immediately trying to get my feet under me and trying to make Ron's vision my own. I met with the various departments to see what they were doing and how I could help. What I found was a self-sufficient staff at every level, highly motivated and effective. They were friendly and cordial, but certainly didn't need much help from me. I visited the sick and shut-ins, a ministry I loved and felt very comfortable with. I attended board meetings and found the men on the board sincere and eager to see the church grow. I was told of the glory days when Westside was attended by thousands and had outreaches all over the Quad Cities, of when famed pastor Tommy Barnett was pastor and many souls were saved. There seemed to be expectancy in the air that those days might return under Ron's leadership.

Ron was a gifted preacher who excelled in the pulpit ministry. He was a great guy with a big heart, loved to study, and cared deeply about the things of God. His sermons were always enthusiastic and vivacious. He was weak, however, in building meaningful relationships and maintained a "professional distance" that made it hard to get to know him at a deeper level. On the other hand, I excelled at relationships and the way I cared for people pastorally. I enjoyed getting to know them and was able to speak into their lives. I was touchable and rarely relied on a "professional distance" as a tool in ministry. Together we could have been a great compliment to each other, and I had high expectations for what could be, but one surprise trumped much that could have been. Unbeknownst to Ron or I, the friend who had helped us find the house in Parkview and who had wanted the position that I had taken was undermining my relationship with Ron, playing us both against each other. Ron began to distrust me and me him. I began to long for a deeper relationship than he could provide.

I had never experienced a friend's betrayal, one who took my words, twisted them, and used them to forge his own agenda. He did the same thing to Ron, and it became an almost unbearable situation. What was created through this undermining in our relationship was a "disconnect" that could not be bridged, and Ron felt it deeply, and so did I.

One day Ron came in my office and said, "You're not happy here, are you?"

I responded, "No, I'm not. I'm miserable."

Through a long conversation, we began to see what was happening and its evil intent. Though we made strides at reconciling the rift created, we never fully recovered from it. As the months passed, things only became dicier. The relational disconnect made it impossible to productively work together. Added to that, there were some rumblings of dissatisfaction in the congregation as well. A deacon had tried to force Ron into resigning because of some personality conflicts he had with him; that deacon was reprimanded, and he was forced to resign. These were tense days indeed that seemed to drag on and on. Time alone never really has the power to heal the hurt of a friend's betrayal. The psalmist David speaks to this unbearable pain when he says, "For it is not my enemy that reproaches me, then I could beat it; nor is it he who hates me who has exalted himself against me . . . But it is you, a man my equal, my companion and my familiar friend" (Psalms 55:12, 13).

Even so, the ministry went forward, and Ron assigned me to teach the book of Revelation on Wednesday nights so he could spend time with the youth ministry. This breathed life into me, and I marveled at the reception my teaching received. In addition, I rallied some of the youth to begin a ministry to a geriatric, mentally handicapped, nursing home in town, a ministry we oversaw for most of the time I was there. It was wonderful to watch the youth of our church learn to share their love with these dear people. Some would lead singing, others would "preach," and the rest would just be a friend to the residents. Sunday school and the other educational programs were also strong and vibrant.

In mid-1994, Ron announced that he was leaving to take a position as director of The Fellowship of Christian Athletes at the University of Florida. He had discussed this with me several times. Ron was an athlete himself, having played basketball in college, and the move made perfect sense. He wondered how his leaving would affect me, but I repeatedly told him that if God was in it for him, He was in it for me too. I told him not to worry about me; I was in His capable hands. (In the Assemblies of God churches, it was expected, if not policy, that staff members resign when the senior pastor did, so that the new Senior Pastor could be free to hire who he would want to assist him. Here, Associate Pastors were hired by the Senior Pastor, not the church board as in some other denominations.) My brother Gene had recently moved to Davenport with his family to function as our youth minister. I was more concerned for him than for myself. He was new to the Assemblies and had taken a great risk in uprooting and making such a move.

When Ron left, the board asked me to be Interim Pastor while they sifted through the plethora of candidates for such a respected church. This I enthusiastically did. The first thing I discovered was that the church was deeply in debt, and much of that was unsecured debt to operational providers like the phone and utilities companies. It had acquired a building downtown to house and minister to drug addicts and outcasts, but the payments were a heavy burden that the church could ill afford.

My top priority in those early days was to sell that building and resolve the operational debt that loomed around fifty thousand dollars. We sold buses and other out buildings that were sitting in the church yard, made all of the cuts that were possible, but in the end, we needed a financial miracle. I helped organize a day we called "Debt Freedom Sunday." We promoted it for several weeks, and in the meantime set a budget for the church and a plan to never get in such a position again. I was honest with the congregation and assured them that once the operational debts were paid, the church would be able to move forward unencumbered as it had been over that past five years. The downtown mission building sold, at no profit, to another ministry in town and when Debt Freedom Sunday came, we all had high hopes that God was up to something.

We had categorized different debts that needed to be paid off and posted the amounts of each, some smaller than others. At the end of the service, individuals and families came forward; some paid an entire smaller bill while others contributed toward paying larger ones. When the service was done, I left feeling that we had done what God wanted us to do, honestly presented the need to the people, shored up a budget that was doable and thrifty, and prayed like crazy. At about four o'clock that afternoon, the chairman of the board called me. He and the other deacons had been counting money all day. He asked what I thought had come in. Man of great faith that I am, I thought ten thousand dollars would be awesome. He told me that all the money we had needed had been supplied by God through the hands of a largely blue-collar congregation which had responded to the need. Our joy and relief knew no bounds. That night, I shared what God had done through them and the place was electrified. I didn't preach; what could I have said that would have mattered that night anyway? We sang joyful songs of praise and deliverance, and I remember that service as one of the most meaningful and memorable day in all my days as a pastor.

Buoyed by such great success and response of the people to my leadership, I threw my hat in the ring to be Senior Pastor. Gene and I had talked about the possibilities that might be ours as a team to do something amazing and special at Westside. I met with the board and they too felt that I should have a chance to present myself as Senior Pastor. A date was set, the district superintendent was notified, and I readied myself to speak as a candidate for Senior Pastor. (In the Assemblies of God in Iowa, a pastor needed to be voted in by the congregation with sixty-six percent of the vote.) When the votes were counted, it was too close to call, and a recount was taken. In the end, I had come up about five votes short. We later discovered that some members had stayed away that night assuming I was a shoe in. We also found out that others who had not attended the church in years, and others still whose memberships were there, though they had moved to other churches, had been contacted to come or write in votes against me.

Gene was livid at the manner of the outcome and wanted to inject scripture for a process he felt was unbiblical to start with. He was coming from a Charismatic church framework and had never fully bought into the Assemblies of God way of doing things. For me, the betrayal I felt was indescribable. I was devastated. If you have never known the betrayal of a confidant friend or the conspiracy of a group against you, you can't imagine the unspeakable hurt it can bring. If you have, no description is needed. These wounds leave you weak and wondering where you went wrong, where God was, or why it happened in the first place. I'm sure that anyone who has laid a life on the line knows what I'm talking about. I was hurt with people, and I was hurt with God. Those wounds were the most profound I had ever known. Certainly, a broken neck and its aftermath don't compare to a heart that is broken.

My guess is that Jesus knows the pain better than I ever will. Somehow in His great love, I think he may still feel the loss of Judas, but unlike Him, I wanted nothing more than revenge. I managed to set these emotions aside and tried to contemplate my next move. But I was a wounded soldier with the fresh scars of disappointment and disillusionment resting on my weary breast. And I was mad at God for leading me to that place "like a lamb to the slaughter." I knew the vote meant that I would have to leave Westside; a staff member who had himself wanted to be Senior Pastor would be a liability a new pastor would not want. Within the week, I resigned to the board and made it official before the congregation the following Sunday.

Two things weighed heavily upon my heart. One was the lack of real relationships. It seemed that every move I had made in ministry, starting back with the split at Ocala Christian fellowship, had resulted in a loss of deep personal relationships, where I enjoyed sharing my faith with others who felt the same way as me. Even in seminary, my classmates and I had cultivated simply a situational relationship that only lasted for the days there. They helped me make it through the rigors of theological study at the time, but the friendships didn't hold when those rigors were finished.

Then, as I began working at First Assembly in Ocala, the best I seemed to have was a professional relationship with the ministers on our staff and area ministers in our section. And now, Westside was a new low in personal relationships for me. There, the relationships were merely surface at best, and always strained. With each move, my relationships deteriorated, and now they had been additionally undermined by deception and accusations. I longed for a return to the depth of personal friendships that had been such an important part of my spiritual growth and maturation. I missed and needed and thrived upon the sharpening knife of Christian men who could sharpen my own faith and walk with Jesus. I hungered for a return to that kind of intimate relationship again.

Worse still, I felt betrayed. Here was a core breakdown for me; I felt betrayed by people, but worse than any other, I felt betrayed by God Himself. The pain of disappointment with God at my seminary graduation resurfaced with an amazing sting. That disappointment with God, His not supplying the money for my diploma, was now being replaced, and in its place, I felt that He was untrustworthy. My thoughts reasoned that I had laid my all on the altar for Him, but He was absent in my most trying hours. I wanted to believe He had me in His hands, that He was working His plan for me, though I couldn't see it. But I harbored a hard distrust and seriously wondered if He was even there or if He cared. I was disillusioned and unsatisfied with ministry, spiritually weary and, running on empty.

Nevertheless, I knew I needed a job; I had a family to support, so I pushed those deep feelings aside for the moment and immediately started making plans to leave. I tightened the church budget I had created so the new pastor would have a working copy when he arrived. I looked into the possibility of becoming a school teacher, giving up the idea of ever pastoring a church again, so deep was the hurt. I looked for a "secular" job and found none. In the end, I started sending resumes to churches looking for pastors. During my last Sunday night service, I recounted the blessing the church had been to me and my family, choosing to accentuate the positive, thanked them for loving us, stated some successes we had enjoyed, and left the pulpit. We were given a going-away fellowship, a love offering, and then we left. If God was in control and still leading me, I needed Him to show me what to do. Christmas was approaching; I had no job and wondered what was next.

CHAPTER 14

Bushnell: Death of a Vision

Early in our marriage, Bev and I attended a seminar called "Institute in Basic Youth Conflicts" with speaker Bill Gothard. It was an amazing weeklong event with new insights at every turn. Among these, one stood out above the rest. The title for the session was, "Understanding the Ways of God." Gothard walked through scripture showing how God did things in the lives of biblical characters. He showed the pattern He used with Abraham, Moses, Isaiah, and many others. He spoke about the three ways that God works . . . birth of a vision, death of a vision, in some cases when He really wants to show his divine power, double death of a vision, and finally, supernatural fulfillment of a vision. Though I resonated with the truth of that teaching at the time, my next move would take that truth to a level I could never have anticipated.

By late December, 1994, I had two real prospects in my search for a new church to pastor. Bushnell Assembly of God called and wanted me to come for an interview with their pulpit committee. Arrangements were made, and a date was set. In the meantime, a church in Jacksonville called and wanted to talk to me, too. I set an appointment with them so that I could go both places on the same trip. An excitement at those possibilities began to grow in my heart. Either would have made it possible to be close to Ocala where my widowed mother still lived and where my deep spiritual roots and relationships were. I prayed that one of them would work out.

Bev and I made the trip alone in early January, our kids stayed behind with friends in Davenport. Bushnell is located a mere thirty five miles from Ocala, and we stayed with my mom when we came down for the interview. I snuck down the day of the meeting with my good friend and fellow pastor, Phil Cook and spied out the area. The church was small. I caught a quick peek into the sanctuary and it seemed a typical small church in a small community. I commented to Phil that Bushnell was not the place for me. I have no idea why I felt that way. Though I was sure that I wouldn't take the church if it was offered to me, I followed through with the scheduled meeting. I was looking beyond that interview and was more hopeful about the church in Jacksonville.

As we met the men in the church yard, I felt comfortable and eager to hear their hearts and to share mine. We had a casual dinner at a local spot and then went to the home of one of the men for the formal get together. Almost immediately I felt a kindred spirit with the pulpit committee. They shared about how deeply they had sensed God's presence as they read resumes and talked to candidates. Some cried at the moving of the Father upon them as they had prayed and sought His will for their church. I answered their questions as honestly as I could, and as the meeting progressed, my heart turned toward them, and I felt that God might want me there in spite of my initial impressions. Before we parted that night, I led in prayer that the person God wanted there would be found. I shared with them that I was interested in God's man for the church far more than I wanted to get the position. We cried and embraced, and as we drove from the church grounds that night, Bev and I looked at each other, both feeling a special bond with the men we had just met. We felt that the church may be offered to us, and if it was, we'd accept.

The next day we headed to Jacksonville for the interview there. This church was all I had wanted. Much larger than Bushnell and more in line with our Charismatic bent, they wanted a shepherd who loved to praise the Lord, one who would take them to a new level in teaching and worship. On the surface, it was a great fit, a much better fit than Bushnell. Their facilities were impressive and included an office complex that would be the envy of anyone who became their new pastor. But what it did not give us was the sense of connection and His pleasure, both of which we had strongly felt when we talked to the men in Bushnell, and we left Jacksonville believing even more firmly that God was leading us to pastor Bushnell Assembly. We headed back to Iowa with no sure future, but believing that God would be active in the choices we would make in the near future, and we were hopeful that He would lead us in the way we should go.

In early January, 1995, Bushnell Assembly of God called me to come and preach as a candidate for pastor. We headed to Florida and steadied our hearts for what we were sure was the leading of God. We stayed at the home of a couple in the church. I attended a men's breakfast on Saturday morning and then a church-wide fellowship that night. Sunday morning, I woke early, walked down the country road that stretched for a few miles, and then dressed for church. I preached both the morning and evening services and then waited in a Sunday school classroom as the congregation voted. The pulpit committee came in to let us know that the church had indeed voted us in. We exhaled an excited breath of relief, hugged, and went back to the sanctuary to be presented as the new pastor of the church. I expressed appreciation for the vote of confidence and promised to do my best to live as a true Christian before them, and to lead them as God led me. We rented a house from the former pastor, a large home with five bedrooms right next door to where we had spent the weekend of my candidacy. We returned to Iowa to pack for the move. Our first Sunday in Bushnell would be the last Sunday of January.

We left Iowa on Bev's fortieth birthday and drove a U-Haul to Florida. Upon arrival, many from the church came to help us unload and get set up in our new home. I had a week before I was to start work, and we spent much of that time getting the kids enrolled in school, visiting family and friends in Ocala, and arranging the home into a place where we were comfortable. I prepared a few sermons and met several of the church leaders. Our spirits were high, and I eagerly anticipated my first day as Senior Pastor of Bushnell Assembly of God. The church sign read, "Welcome Brack Family."

I quickly settled into my routine of study and the myriad of things that are required of a new pastor. Members of our church dropped by both the church and our new home to welcome us and offer to help us in any way they could. I inherited a youth pastor and his secretary wife, and they helped me meet a few shut-ins and provided me a small lay of the land. I quickly made acquaintance with a few other local pastors and found them friendly. I longed for relationships with these men and quickly settled down with the pastor of the First Baptist Church, Ken Weaver. Through the next few years, he and I would meet regularly for fellowship and soon became buddies. I was and still am grateful for his genuine love for me and our common goal to see people saved and changed by a dynamic relation with the Father. I sought council from Pastor McDaniel in those early days, feeding on his rich mentoring and the wisdom of his many years of pastoral leadership. Everything seemed well, but things, I was to learn in short order, are rarely what they seem. Within a month, serious conflicts arose.

At my first official board meeting, I began with prayer and started the meeting with a small devotional designed to foster a new relationship with these men who had so recently impressed me with their desire for my style of leadership. I wanted to ask them personal questions about their devotional lives, their needs, and desires. I didn't want, especially at this first meeting, to just discuss budgets and problems. I was eager to talk about accountability to each other as men seeking a deeper walk with the Lord. I was surprised to discover that a few of the men were uncomfortable and they had no desire for this style of "board meeting."

Soon, factions arose with some of the board and others in the church. Some of these as well as other influential members would visit me in my church office and talk about what was going on in the church that they thought "I needed to know." They wanted to inform me of some members' pasts and "help" me "understand things better." I soon realized, according to them, that "many" were unhappy with their new pastor. Their discontent and accusations ran an irrational gamut: I was in my office studying too much, I wasn't in my office enough, I wasn't available for "drop in" visitors, I needed to be out visiting more, I apparently wanted (unbeknownst to me) to get rid of the youth pastor who had faithfully served there many years, people were leaving the church because . . . . the list seemed endless.

On the heels of these things, others, I was informed, were very concerned that I had come to the church under false representation. I was accused of lying on my resume, nonspecific accusations that I misrepresented my pastoral experience as well as other falsehoods I was portraying. The discontentments were voiced one after another so rapidly I could not get my hands around them. In the wake of each one, ministry leaders resigned while congregation members left the church, adding fuel to a fire that was already out of control. I was told that some on the board and other members of the church were calling for a "vote of confidence" and my resignation. One Sunday, many of these things came to a head as a man came forward and point blank told me to admit that I had lied on my resume. I had no idea what he was referring to. Under the weight of accusation, the congregation began to shrink. People I hadn't had time to even meet were leaving. The church board seemed split: some seemed excited about the direction the church was going, and others questioned my every move. As a result, I began what would become a long night of the soul, a time, not for fellowship or seeking God's heart and vision, but questioning my leadership, magnifying my mistakes and missteps, and haggling over money, people, and more specifically, my leadership style. I had only been at the church three months.

As we labored through the spring of 1995, I determined that I would try to outlast the discontent and weather the storm. I felt such conviction that God had called me to the church that we decided to get out of the temporary rental arrangement and buy a home. We found a place that was smaller but still comfortable for the six of us and set out to stay for the long haul. I was determined to lead the church as best I could and make a real "go" of pastoring a small church in a small community where everyone knew everyone, and had for generations.

Most painful of all was the toll being exacted on my family, specifically my four impressionable children. They were young and in a new community that was skeptical of outsiders. Being the new kids on the block, they would become the innocent front line soldiers in battles they hadn't chosen, and about which they had no comprehension. Their activities, choices of clothing, behavior, even their friendships were not only questioned, but brought into board meetings where some seemed bent on getting rid of us.

Amidst a flood of difficulties, my youth pastor who had been a part of the church staff for several years resigned, which only added fire to an already rampant skepticism. I brought on a young college graduate from Zion Bible College to take the vacant position. He, too, experienced the discontent of the church board. While we tried to forge a new vision for our youth ministry and the church as a whole, we seemed to meet resistance at every turn. Before long, we both intuitively knew that our time at Bushnell Assembly was limited. I encouraged him to begin to look for other opportunities and to let it be known through our denominational contacts that he was looking for another church.

Sometime around the spring of 1997, spiritually dry and at my wits' end, I decided to take a trip to Pensacola to visit Brownsville Assembly of God, where a true revival was in full swing. The revival had attracted crowds from all over the world and Evangelist Steve Hill was the keynote speaker in meetings that were held six days a week. I had no real preconceived ideas about what I might experience there, and, to be honest, I held little expectation that anything remarkable would happen that would help me. I could not have been more wrong. What I experienced in those two days revived my soul and initiated a whole new personal freedom.

The evangelist spoke the first night with such conviction and brokenness on the topic, "I See Weeds." He used the example of how the weed Kudzu takes over and eats away trees and vegetation, often leaving behind a beautiful green exterior while it does so. It looks good from a distance, but underneath is a destructive force that is as devastating as a swarm of locusts. He hadn't spoken long before I was under such conviction I could barely control my emotions. I began to weep as I saw the Kudzu of my own spiritual life. Every word spoken pierced me to the core, and all I could see were the "weeds" of my own life. The many attempts at planting a beautiful life had steadily grown into a destructive façade, and I felt its pain deeper than I can put into words. That night I wept great sobs of pain and repentance, sobs more a groaning from the depths of my soul than any emotional experience in my life.

I went back to my motel room only to weep deeper still. I don't know how long I cried into the night. I wept for my children, I wept for my wife, I wept for my ministry, I wept for my soul. Deep groaning engulfed me at the core of my being as I wept, wave after wave of hurt and failure and disappointment consuming me. Sometime in the night I fell into a deep sleep, no dreams, no visions, just deep sleep.

When I awoke the next morning, I felt clean. The dawn, after that long night of agony and the deep sleep that followed it, renewed me. I felt new, brand new. Gone were my feelings of despair and failure. Gone were the hopelessness and helplessness I had carried for so long. I felt a new sense of vision and purpose, and my heart was clean, really clean.

I was to meet Bev in Mississippi that night to see my brother and spend a few hours with him and his wife before we headed back to Bushnell. I stopped to get a cold drink for the trip. I entered a rundown convenience store and purchased a cold bottle of Mountain Dew. As I climbed back into the car and began driving, I noticed that something else had changed during that agonizing night.

Hebrews 12: 1 says, ". . . let us lay aside every encumbrance and the sin which so easily entangles us, and let us run with endurance the race that is set before us . . ." I have always thought that we humans are encumbered in our spiritual lives and that many times we have a particular sin that "so easily entangles us." Many times, as I have heard that verse quoted or as I simply read it myself, many times even when I preached from that text, I would fall under conviction because I knew the sin, the particular sin that so easily entangled and trapped me. Since as far back as I can remember, pornography was the sin that entangled me.

From my earliest youth it had plagued my personal life and more importantly, the life I knew that Christ wanted for me. In my preteen years, while innocently walking through the woods, I came upon a heap of adult magazines. Mesmerized, I turned page after page, my mind taking snapshots of each scene. As a teenager, I worked as a stock boy for a convenience store. In the stock room were stacks of pornographic magazines to be shelved or disposed of, and again I would be mysteriously drawn to them, standing long moments staring at forbidden images that attached themselves to my psyche. As a young Marine, free from the restraints of parents and away from home, I indulged myself in the ready opportunities to feed a growing habit. Even after committing my life anew to Christ and surrendering to His call to ministry, I still would sneak peeks at material that should have disgusted me.

As time moved on, I began to gain more control of the urges to taste the forbidden fruit. Disgusted with myself and desperate to rid myself of this "entanglement," I became more accountable to a fellow struggler and built real safeguards that kept me victorious. Though I had occasional slip-ups that often descended upon me like a surprise attack (Pearl Harbor comes to mind; I even called my attacks "being Japped"), for the most part I had found victory in my long battle. I praised God for His victory, believing that, while I would always struggle with this entangling sin, He had made a way of escape, even victory, for me. The idea that one can be totally set free from such an entangling sin was neither a part of my belief system nor my wildest dream.

But as I began to drive away from that convenience store on my way to Mississippi that sunny day, I stopped in my tracks. I realized that I had entered a store, bought a cold drink, paid the man behind the counter, and walked out the door without using one of my most basic safeguards against pornography. That safeguard was to make a covenant with my eyes and to deliberately turn my gaze away from pornography. This new day, this day preceded by a long night of weeping and repentance, I hadn't used that safeguard because I didn't need it. That morning I realized that I had not walked in just victory, I had found freedom.

I can't explain it and I sure don't understand why it happened to me, of all people. I felt like the blind man who Jesus healed. His only response was, "How, I don't know (I would add, why, I don't know). One thing I do know, that though I was blind, now I see" (Jn. 9:25). I felt the same way. Once I was stuck in an entangling sin over which the best that I could do was struggle to keep a measure of victory. But now I was free. Many aspects of that night of weeping have come and gone from my life, but this is my story: From that day in the spring of 1997 until this moment right now some fourteen plus years later, I have never even been tempted with pornography again, and I have lived not just victorious over it, but totally free from it. And this freedom has lasted. To anyone struggling with any "entangling sin," I say that victory is wonderful and far greater than defeat, but victory doesn't hold a candle to freedom, glorious freedom. I am forever grateful to His amazing grace and power that set me free.

One night after coming home from that trip to Brownsville and the personal renewal and freedom I found there, I lay in bed thanking the Father for once again rescuing me from myself. I quietly whispered to Bev, "I was ready to give up."

Bev's tender response was simply, "I know."

I whispered quieter still, "I don't mean just church or ministry. I mean on God." As I drifted off to sleep that night, I was unaware how prophetic those words were.

The revival at Brownsville also gave me great hope for the ministry at Bushnell Assembly. I began to pray more and trust God to move in the church. I committed myself to regular times of prayer and wanted to lead the church to become a praying church. I started a Tuesday night prayer service which was attended by just a few, but I was buoyed with expectation, knowing that often God begins with a small band, and from that, I felt certain He would bring revival to our church. I even began to talk about expanding our facilities for the coming move of God there. I preached inspired messages that came from God's heart. I was no longer content with just preaching sermons. My heart cried to hear His voice and communicate His heart to the church. I was eager to be a conduit for the Spirit's moving in my heart and in the life of Bushnell Assembly of God.

Even so, before long the board meetings digressed into complaints about the way the church was going. Before long, the spirit of division and discontent that was the hallmark of my ministry there resurfaced. My youth pastor took a position elsewhere with my blessing, and I wondered what I could do to change the stalemate that had been the norm for practically my whole time there.

Bev became more involved with the ministries at Bushnell Assembly. She led the youth ministry, was a leader on the worship team, and coached Bible Quiz, a denominational ministry where youth would compete with other youth in scripture quotation and theological concepts. While I was dying from the struggles that consumed me, she thrived in her new found place in ministry. Her love affair with Christ that had always seemed to dwarf my own was amazing. She came into her own, and I soon saw her as the vital help that I needed. We complimented each other in ways we had never before enjoyed. She seemed on fire. The fire within my own soul seemed to be slowly but surely dying out.

When we had first come to the church, Bev was attacked by some because she didn't seem interested in being a part of this or that ministry. No one seemed to care that she was busy raising our four kids and didn't have time to run to every meeting that pastor wives were supposed to attend. At board meetings, I would be queried about why she wasn't more involved with the church ministries, especially some of the women's ministries. Now she was being attacked because she was too involved. We became convinced that the problem lay not with us, but with a leadership team that simply wanted us to go.

This is not to say that every board member or every experience at Bushnell Assembly was against us. There was the time when the men of our church attended a Promise Keepers conference and we all were deeply touched by God. Two men carried me from the arena on their shoulders and proclaimed me "a man of God." There were many conversations with members that were so meaningful and deep that both they and I cried under the weight of His divine presence. Others would talk to me about God's call on their own lives and asked me to talk and pray with them about important spiritual decisions they were making. Others were so faithful in their service to me, the church, and the Lord; they blessed me over and over. Some were so faithful in the weekly prayer meetings I had started, their enthusiasm often outshined my own and brought courage to my soul. New people came to the church, attracted by my teaching style and loved the church and me. There were men's retreats that fostered new human relationships and wonderful encounters with the divine presence.

Even with so many great things happening, my psyche was so damaged by the vocal few that I saw very little hope for my future as a pastor at Bushnell Assembly or anywhere else for that matter. I began to have serious doubts in my personal leadership abilities and any naysayer could pretty much unnerve and rattle me to the core. When I should have "taken the bull(s) by the horns," I was too weak and so self-doubting in my leadership decisions that I was unable to stand tall and firm. This was my own character flaw, and while others exploited it, it is my own fault for not being more resolute in my pastoral leadership. I coped as best as I could, waiting for a divine deliverance to arrive.

In the meantime, I continued my faithful preaching and teaching ministry, visiting the sick, burying the dead, counseling, reaching out into the community through the local ministers' association and various outreaches of my own church, and, sadly, hoping more than praying that the Lord would turn things around, or at least show me what to do.

As the summer of 1999 was coming to an end, Bev, who was leading the youth ministry at the time, and I decided we wanted to take the youth on a spiritual retreat. We made plans to go to the mountains where my brother, Gene, would lead a spiritual retreat designed to challenge the youth to a deeper dimension in the Lord. The day before we were to leave, two of my board members announced that they would go along for the trip, saying they were concerned that we didn't have enough adult supervision in place. Bev and I both felt they were coming to keep an eye on us, and we were highly offended at this development.

When we returned, one of my board members let me know that the deacons had started an early Morning Prayer meeting on Sunday mornings. I was told I was welcome to come if I wanted. Warily, I began coming to the six o'clock prayer time. We'd pray silently for a time and then, one by one, each would pray. It seemed spontaneous and I appreciated the fact that they were praying for the church and for me, but I couldn't help but think this prayer time came with an unspoken agenda. I felt uncomfortable praying with these leaders who didn't seem interested in praying any other time and all things considered didn't do much to bolster any ministry in the church. All the while, I was steadily dying in a free fall I could neither understand nor control. I knew my time as pastor of Bushnell Assembly had run its course and would soon be coming to an end, I just didn't know how or when.

In late October, I attended a Sectional Ministers meeting outside Ocala. Pastor McDaniel, the minister who had mentored me in my first full-time ministry position and now was the Sectional Presbyter over the Assemblies of God churches in the area, pulled me aside after the meeting. He told me that one of my board members had contacted him asking how they could get rid of me. I felt embarrassed and ashamed that he had been contacted and been placed in the dubious and uncomfortable position of brokering the discontent and troubles some of the church leadership had with me. At the same time, I was glad he was my friend, and I had full confidence in him. Pastor McDaniel is a man of God who is so gentle and caring, and I was glad he was going to walk with me through this time.

A meeting with the deacon board was arranged. Pastor McDaniel met with me and the board, and then I went to the church to sit in my office and wait for whatever information or fate awaited me. Their meeting lasted about forty-five minutes after which Pastor McDaniel met me at the church. The board had agreed to pay me through the end of the year, but wanted my resignation immediately. Pastor and I went back and met with the board, we hugged, I submitted my resignation effective in two weeks, and I went home.

The following Sunday I read my resignation to the church. Some wept as I announced I was leaving, an honest display of affection from those quiet supporters who saw the good I had tried to bring. A week later, I preached for the last time followed by dinner on the grounds. I had packed my office up the week before, and I was more than ready to leave. I wasn't sure what I was going to do for work, but I had made up my mind that "ministry" had seen the last of me. I'd refuse to put my kids, my wife, or myself in that position again. The toll exacted is hard to express. The disappointment I felt with God through these trying years was inconsolable. The knife of constant pressure had slowly slashed the vestiges of my calling to ministry. The loss of my self-worth was complete, and I could barely hold my head above water. For the years I had invested in full-time Christian work, I was bankrupt. The Bible says that "If one can overpower him who is alone, two can resist him. A cord of three strands is not quickly torn apart" (Eccl. 4:12). I felt overpowered and alone. I had no relationships that could help me weather this storm. My close spiritual relationships seemed so far away. And worst, God Himself with His redemptive tenderness seemed to have forsaken me. The cords of my life were frayed at best, broken entirely at worst. I had lost confidence in my ability to make even the most simple of decisions. Among the many conflicting emotions I remember from that day was relief. In a way I felt a weight was being lifted off my shoulders.

The birth of a vision of my childhood when I felt the Divine tug, the birth of a vision when I first realized his call in my heart, the birth of a vision when I was visited again and again through encounters with His presence had slowly led me to death: Death of the vision of church work, death of the vision of the pastoral. Death of the vision that He even knew me at all, death of the vision that I was really in His hands, death of the vision that faith in Him was real or worthwhile, death of the vision that He would provide the money for my seminary diploma, death of the vision for Westside Assembly. Death! I had gloriously embraced God's birth of a vision repeatedly throughout my life. Death of a vision was a bitter, soul-wrenching mixture of personal failures and Satan's faithful reminders dug from the bowels of Hell, and a God who didn't seem present to rebut them.

I know now that years before that last service, slowly at first, but gaining speed at every turn, I had begun dying. With each new conflict, each new problem, each new criticism, I had died a little. Disillusion with ministry and, more importantly, my own "subterraneous suspicions of God," were sabotaging both my faith in Him and myself. I felt He had led me to the slaughter and my own personal ineptness had finished the job. By the time I walked out of the church that Sunday afternoon, I was relieved . . . and lost. Sadness and uncertainty would soon follow, but that day I was glad that an almost five year ordeal would soon be over, or so I thought.

CHAPTER 15

Rest in Peace

In 1991, a movie came out called *City Slickers*, a story about a couple of friends who went on a cattle drive vacation on a dude ranch, fulfilling a lifelong dream. The movie was a comedy that carried a range of serious subplots showing the importance of friendship and centering on the meaning of what fulfills a person's life. There is a scene in the movie when the two friends were talking, and one turned to the other and asked, "What was the best day of your life?"

The other responded, "The day my father finally left my mother." Evidently the father had been abusive and hard on his family, and as a result, the son had felt that it was best that his father left both he and his mother alone and in peace.

Then his friend asked him, "What was the worst day of your life?"

The friend's response was shocking in its direct portrayal of his feelings. Spoken in a contemplative tone he simply said, "The same day."

Those scripted words sum up my feelings of the day I left pastoral ministry. I was so glad to finally be free from the rigors that had become misery more than ministry. I had started out with such hope and excitement. Each new day had, in the beginning, offered the promise of reaching out and touching people, sometimes in their most desperate moments. I had visited the sick with such purity and intentional love. I had often preached soul-stirring and heartfelt messages. I had connected with brothers and sisters in the excitement of the love of Christ. The day I entered into vocational full-time Christian work was in some ways the best day of my life. I was finally doing what I had felt so strongly for so long was the call of God on my life. But as time went on and I dealt with problems without solutions, accusations that often loomed larger and more pressing than any ministry I might have to offer, and self doubts produced by real and imagined weaknesses, I began to loathe the fact that I'd ever entered Christian work at all. As I looked back, I felt that the day I entered full time Christian service may have been not only the best day of my life, but also the worst day of my life. Like the character in the movie—"Same day."

My first days of "freedom" were a mix of emotions. Freedom! No longer was there the ever-present sermon to prepare that took many hours of study and preparation and felt like a universe of its own hanging over my head. Freedom from the Saturday nights' restless sleep produced by the anxiety I always felt about standing in front of a crowd and trying to tell them about a God who is in fact beyond words. No longer would I have to face the board meetings where it seemed that my every move, or lack thereof, was scrutinized and critiqued. No longer would I feel the weight of a discontented parishioner who had announced that He was leaving the church because of . . . well, you can fill in the blank. No longer would I have the constant soul searching through each conflict, large or small, and wondering where I had missed God's best intentions for me or the church and the many "what ifs" and "I should haves" that accompany such times of deep introspection. No longer would I have to change family plans or stay in touch with a church while on vacations and outings because of "business" matters. No longer would my kids be subjected to unfair treatment simply because they were "the preacher's kids." Freedom! Yes indeed, that freedom made my last day in ministry seem like the best day of my life.

But there was another emotion that also surfaced as I stepped away from church work, and its burden tormented my mind for many, many months. Failure! I was a failure at the only endeavor at which I had so wanted to be a success. I started ministries that never really realized the potential I had envisioned. Sunday school classes stagnated, church attendance dropped, attempts at creating an atmosphere where everyone felt loved and cared for eluded me. Sermons came and went in a blur, never seeming to really catch root in the hearts that needed it most. Though I have had a pretty serious wrestling match with "Old Man Failure" most of my life, this time he seemed to grow horns and tails like the apocalyptic beast of Revelation. Its thorny horns and soul-stinging tail set its aim at permanently branding me. I may be overstating the truth a little, but that is what I felt deep in my bones. And leaving the church that November day seemed to vie for the worst day of my life.

Best day of my life? Worst day of my life? An argument could be made that it was "the same day."

Pastor McDaniel tried to encourage me to not give up on the ministry. He seemed to think that I had just tried to fit in a church setting that was out of my gift mix, and he punctuated his point by offering me little places to preach, hoping that the latent "itch" of ministry would kick back in and I'd be fine. Certainly, his forty-plus years in pastoral ministry gave him far better insight into the ebb and flow of church work than I had. So at his bidding, I preached in a small church outside of Ocala the Sunday after my last day at Bushnell Assembly. What he didn't know, and what I didn't know at the time, was that I was dead inside and done with church.

I don't blame anyone or any church, but the truth was I just didn't feel that I even wanted to continue with the ministry as I had been experiencing it. Some might say that I was burned out. Some might say that I just needed a sabbatical. Whatever one might call it, I was done, finished. My life was drained, my spirit crushed under a weight I couldn't understand and was simply unwilling to carry any more.

Before long, my desire to even attend church was gone. It felt weird for Sunday to come around and not have to go to church. At first I felt guilty for sitting on my front porch swing as others on our street who knew I had been a "preacher" would see me swinging away in my shorts and t-shirt as they themselves headed off to church somewhere. For a while I was embarrassed when Christians would ask where we went to church. I would pass the ball as best I could and walk away. The truth was, I felt that by going to church I was playing a game I didn't want to play anymore, trying to act like everything was great, when it was not. I was emotionally spent, physically exhausted, disillusioned with "ministry," mad at God . . . and if that wasn't enough, in the deepest possible meaning, I was spiritually dead.

I needed a full and complete change. I approached the school board, looking for an opportunity, any opportunity to change my vocation and thereby restore myself to some semblance of life. I was hired to teach students who needed extra help with passing the FCAT, a Florida's state exam that all students must pass to graduate. With the New Year, 2000, I found myself teaching writing skills to middle and high school students.

The change was dramatic, but I felt so relieved to be out of the public eye and working in a place where I was free from the myriad difficulties I had known in ministry.

From time to time over the first three years of teaching, my work would change. As I pulled students to give them extra help, many teachers either forgot or merely wouldn't send them to me. There were days when I had no students at all. I'd sit alone in the empty room to which I was assigned, alone with a computer and time. Time was something I had not had much of the past few years. Well, I'd had time, but I was unable to relax, to breathe, and unwind. I had been under constant pressure for so long I never was able to get enough rest to feel rejuvenated. Suddenly, I had a lot of time.

My work required such little effort I felt guilty for even being paid. Sometimes, no, many times, when no students came, I'd sit staring into space, in a daze. I remember looking out the windows of my classroom and mindlessly staring into the distance, past the next classroom, past the football field, past the school grounds. I'd be lost in empty thoughts, wandering around a make believe world where I loved life, and all was well. Sometimes these "trips" were not into happy places. At times I'd find myself back in the Marines in scary situations and dark fear and regret would grab me from behind. Fortunately, these mindless visits into La-La land, good or bad, would often be interrupted by a student or administrator checking on me. It wasn't that I was losing my mind or touch with reality. It was more that my need to empty myself of the baggage of disillusionment and disappointment was more acute that I had ever realized.

Soon, my family and I settled into routines that did not center around or involve church work or attendance. Our weekends were free, so we took full advantage of short trips. We began to reconnect with old friends. We quickly realized that our time was our own. Nights were spent doing nothing or anything. But I was not well. A trip to the doctor confirmed that my weight was a problem. I was fifty pounds overweight, and he told me that I should lose those pounds or plan to die earlier than I should.

I started a diet that included riding a stationary bicycle thirty minutes a day. As the weight came off my body, my heart remained heavy in spirit. I didn't pray or read the Bible, and I didn't trust the God I had tried to serve all my life. I was under no particular compulsion or conviction about my spiritual condition, and for the first time I can remember I felt nothing of the passion I had known for Him or His people. Bev and I no longer talked into the night about Him or what He might want. Those had been the topics of so many late-night chats that its absence was its only presence. A deep spiritual numbness was all I felt. I became cynical about anything related to my former life with Him. I was leery and skeptical when hanging around old friends who seemed enamored with the Lord, even fearful they might query me about where I was spiritually—which was nowhere. From time to time I'd attend church services, but even then, I was not truly there. I felt nothing!

As time passed, I enjoyed being with my children and watching them grow and change. John and Philip were home and struggling with things teenagers often struggle with, school pressures with their relational roller coasters and academic pressures, and trying to figure out who they were and where they were going. Where I'd once offered "God's plan for their lives," now I only offered the normal pat answers that most parents give: I wanted them to be productive members of society. Whether they chose God's plan or not didn't really matter to me. I didn't trust Him for my own life, and I didn't try to peddle Him on them or steer them to trust Him either. Philip entered the Air Force and John waged his own wars through high school.

Joseph, my oldest son, had gone in the Air Force as I was going through the last throes with Bushnell Assembly. He was married and doing well, living in Texas as I was in my spiritual slumbers. Christy, my only daughter, finished high school and moved to St. Petersburg for school and work. I'd visit them often, and from time to time attend a church service. But there was no denying the fact that I was through with "church."

Gradually, I began to bounce back from the physical exhaustion that had resulted from the stress of church work. My friends never questioned me as I thought they would. They seemed to instinctively know that I was not ready for such a conversation. We took ballroom dancing lessons and enjoyed social get-togethers, but spiritual subjects were never broached or discussed. Whether this was planned or not, I don't know, but it was exactly what I needed to restore me and help me recover from the emotional strain I felt from my perceived ministerial failures.

In the darkness of night, when no one was there and I was alone with my thoughts, I'd think of God. I no longer thought of serving Him or even wanting to. Gone was the wonder and passion I had felt so many times and which had driven me to pursue Him with my whole life. Absent too was even a flicker of light or hunger for what I had once had with Him. I still believed in Him and I knew He was real, but I felt no spiritual pulse or desire to try to rekindle any relationship with Him. The truth is I was mad at Him. I thought that I had given my all and that He had crushed me in return. I had followed His lead, and He had led me to a dead end. The inspiration He had initiated had left me spiritually disillusioned and spent. In short, I felt He had toyed with me, and I was tired of His "game." (I write this now and know how wrong I was. I dare say that many a Christian has come to this point at some time in their walk with Him.)

As time continued to pass, I was recovering physically. My health was better than it had been in fifteen years. I walked regularly, rode the stationary bike, and even started playing tennis again. I was no longer so exhausted, and I enjoyed coming home from work to cooking supper, something I had never done. I was better emotionally, too. I seemed to be thriving in the school system, one year even selected as Teacher of the Year at my school. I had found something that I was pretty good at, and it didn't drain my life the way church work had. The anger I had strongly felt so long about people in church who had hurt me or who I thought had done me wrong began to abate and I was gradually healing at an emotional level. Bev and I were still deeply in love, and in some ways our marriage was better than it had been in years. We spent all our free time together, reconnecting with old friends and just having fun. Our relationship was as good as ever, except one thing: the spiritual aspect, once the prevalent lynchpin of our lives, was gone. She was still alive, I was dead.

CHAPTER 16

Proof of Life

During my first year at Baptist Bible Institute, I was required to study the "Inter-biblical period," a span of about four hundred years when there was no prophetic voice in the Hebrew nation. That period of time has been called by many names, one of which is "the four hundred years of silence." The profound absence of the booming prophetic voice once so prevalent in Israel was no more, and its absence, though in terms of human history was but a breath, would be called "silence." This so-called silence is a misnomer because God has never stopped communicating and reaching out to His people. The nation of Israel was to ruminate and remember the great prophetic word while looking for the promised Messiah. The four hundred years of "silence" caused Israel to not only look for the Messiah, but long for His presence and voice again. In my life, I was experiencing that silence, but not it's longing. Not yet.

I had preached so many sermons, attended seminars and spiritual pep rallies. I had seen and heard of God's moving among His people. My own personal history is rich with His thundering voice, a small sample of which is included in this writing. Of course, He was not always loud. I have known wonderful times of what seemed like special visitations from Him that gave strength and encouragement to me in the quietness of my own heart, inaudible but more real than the thunder. In fact, most times His was a soft voice, a presence that comforted me in sorrow, and girded me with might for the battles of my life. I remember precious times when I read the Bible and passages leapt from the page with such power they captivated my entirety. His spirit wooed and hovered over me with gentle breezes, reassuring me that I was His. The river of His presence, flowing grace and mercy and love, was real to me, precious to me, and it had been my lifelong comfort and steady guide. But now—now there was no sound at all.

Sometimes my religious habits drew me to try again, and I'd open the Bible, but all I could do was stare at meaningless, lifeless pages of ink. At meals I would go through the ritual of saying a blessing, a prayer I had repeated for years, my lips moving, my voice audible, but my spirit dumb, my heart dark with silence. Other times I would visit family or friends and attend worship services with them, but I sat untouched by the message, uninterested in the point, unchanged by the experience, and seemingly deaf to the sound of His voice. I kept no journal, I wrote no record of this time in my life, and writing it now I cannot do it justice. I don't know if my words can ever adequately convey the lostness I felt and experienced, as the days and the years just rolled by.

I am a sinner. I've always been a sinner. I've done so many things for which I am embarrassed and ashamed. Some of these have produced a 'great sadness' in my soul. But a new sadness now gripped me, a sadness I had never known. It wasn't a situational sadness that a change in situation would fix. It wasn't a financial sadness; even winning the lottery wouldn't fix it. It wasn't a human sadness; friends and earthly relationships were powerless to fix it. It wasn't even just another of many "dark nights of the soul" where the morning would come, or a few days pass, and all would be well again. I could not pull myself up by my proverbial bootstraps: It seemed that once again Humpty Dumpty had taken a great fall, and all of the king's horses and all of the king's men couldn't put this Humpty back together again. This great sadness didn't make me feel worthless or make me want to commit suicide as others' sadness had. This sadness was about a deep, hollow silence of a voice I had heard since my childhood, beckoning me to follow and assuring me of grace. And in its absence, nothing else filled me, nothing else really mattered.

Soon, a feeling of dread began to grow in me. Since I had never experienced such a prolonged period of time without some sense of the divine presence, I felt that I had perhaps crossed a line, and I began to seriously doubt that I had ever truly been in His hands at all. I had no unction to dispel the feeling that I had lost my salvation entirely. Though I had been taught most of my life and had believed in the doctrine of eternal security, and though I still believed that God existed and was real, I could not dispel this feeling of doubt. In pastoral ministry, I had more than once counseled people who had felt that they had lost their salvation. I had shared scriptures and prayed with them, trying to help them through what I thought was simply a "crisis of faith." As I found myself in that exact situation, I discovered that my counsel had been grossly inept and shallow and had trivialized the deep crisis they were going through, and though I tried to buoy my soul with my own counsel, telling myself that we walk by faith not by sight (or in my case feelings) I now experientially knew, at a personal level, the deep despair that must have gripped them because that despair now had a vice grip on me. A few nights during this time, I would broach this topic with Bev. I asked her if she had ever felt that way. She said no. I asked her if she thought I had lost my salvation, she said no. She asked me what I felt, and I told her the truth. I felt nothing at all.

For the most part, I kept this agonizing dread to myself. One night Bev and I were talking, and after a long silence Bev said, "You know what I miss? I miss the spiritual man I married." She missed the spiritual dynamic of our lives. She sensed me balking and quickly added, "I don't mean church or the ministry. I just miss Jesus being the center of our lives." There was no condemnation or accusation in her words, no blame rendered, no fault meant. Just a simple truth that He was not what He had always been to us. I had no answer, and her remarks made me neither better nor worse. I kissed her on the cheek, rolled over, and mindlessly fell asleep.

With the passage of time, this dread became more pronounced. I began to tell Bev about it and often sought reassurance from her. She remained steady as always, and prayed quiet prayers for me. She confided in her close friend about what I was going through, and she, too, joined in praying for me. This was unbeknownst to me at the time, but I did know that I was powerless to change myself. One night I came across a "YouTube" video of a young preacher speaking at a youth conference. Rev. Paul Washer decried the shallow salvation that many young people in churches across the country were experiencing, a conversion without real repentance and change. He persuasively built the case for Godly repentance evidenced by real change in the heart and behavior. He was from the tried and true "old school," where the penitent tarried long and prayed through until, as John Wesley, the great preacher and founder of the Methodist church would say, "the heart was strangely warmed." While his point was well-made and important, it only added to my dread. I knew despite Bev's and others' assurance to the contrary, I was lost and that I would stand alone on that great day to face the judgment of God. The thought scared me to death. The preacher's message brought little comfort to me, for I felt no tug of the Spirit, no conviction, and no repentance. I'd never felt more utterly alone in my life.

I made no pretense of being anywhere other than where I was. I'd keep living and doing the best that I could. Strangely, other areas of my life were going well. I continued to enjoy teaching and having the time with my family I hadn't had during my years in church work. I always looked forward to seeing my lifelong friends, as we learned to dance and laughed at each other doing it. We met with these couples regularly and had dinner and relaxing day trips to the beach or other recreational areas. We even went on wonderful vacations with them. These were outlets for me and they provided a temporary reprieve from the gnawing feeling deep within. But the respite was not strong enough to carry me through the darkness that seemed to be getting darker all the time.

One night as we lay in bed, Bev made a declaration that would set a new course, though I didn't see it at the time. She wasn't mean-spirited but she was emphatic. "It's time to get over it and move on." She was of course referring to my disillusionment with ministry and disappointment with God, to my hurt with church people and my many perceived failures. It had been better than seven years since I had left church work, and it was time. She was right, as she often is, but I couldn't move. I was stuck in a place I'd never been, fighting battles I'd never fought, and dismay was my constant friend. I hadn't prayed or read the Bible with any spirit for so long I seriously doubted I ever would again.

Just as my darkness and its accompanying silence was at its greatest point, our dear friends Lamar and Cliffette began to seriously ask me about teaching the book of Revelation in their home. They had asked about this several times before and I had effectively brushed the request aside. Over the years of my church work, I had led a Bible study of the book several times, and I knew two immutable truths about teaching it. One was that it was a rich study and it evoked interest from every angle. My presentation had always been different from the main interpretations and concentrated on its practical applications for our lives today. The other truth was that to teach it required a relationship with its author. Simply put, the teacher of this book had to be alive. I was not. I was sure that I was in no shape to tackle this magnificent book with these wonderful people.

Undeterred in their gentle but persistent request, their family was eager to delve into the Revelation. And they wanted me, of all people, to be the one to lead the study. I felt that all my good friends had conspired against me, and I finally relented and told them I would do it. We set a beginning date and time, January of 2007. We'd meet every other Thursday night. Even as I acquiesced, I immediately regretted being talked into it. I was a valley of dry bones tackling a book that demanded a full head and a full heart. I had the information in my notes and the basic concepts in my head. I had taught it enough times to wing most of its major divisions. What I didn't have was heart. I was losing the battle of my life and trying to just keep the great dread waging a war inside me at bay. I had no life within, and hadn't even opened a Bible in months. My prayer life had been reduced to a faithless, emotionless sigh, "God help me."

I tried to back out. I tried to postpone. But I was stuck. With no faith, no fire, no passion, and no life, I began. The first night of the study, I asked the little group two questions. I'd asked these questions every time I had begun the study before and I was following that rote script. The first question was, "Why do you want to study the Book of Revelation?" The replies were similar to other settings in which I had taught and everyone wanted to understand the book better. The second question was more poignant. "Why do you want me to teach you the book?" I don't remember the responses to that question. My own mind elaborated on the question itself. "What qualified me of all people to teach this book to those who were far more Christian than me? " I was no more worthy to lead this small group of giants than to lead the armies of the nations. "Don't you know that I am dead?" The hypocrisy I felt was palatable and I couldn't believe I would actually be able to fake my way through. And I was faking my way, prompting a new fear to grip my already empty heart. They would surely find out what my own bankrupt heart had been telling me for a long time: I was lost, truly, irretrievably lost, and that fact would soon be plain to them too.

With this trepidation, I began leading the study of the book of Revelation. The first few weeks I covered background information, nothing too profound as I eased my way through. This part required little passion, and it was a good thing, I had none. A tape recorder was placed near me to document the study. We then would walk through the text, introduction and the Seven Churches. As I presented week after week, my heart condemned me further as I saw the words of Jesus addressed to the seven churches. I explained as best I could "the good, the bad, and the ugly," and constantly saw myself in the latter. This was going to be more difficult than even I had imagined. Yet, week after week, as we discussed the texts, my 'students' were active listeners, interjecting their own thoughts and observations, and graciously encouraging me, telling me how good the study was. Though it felt good to be encouraged in this way, I took their compliments with a grain of bitter salt.

In the time between the teaching appointments, I found myself in my study, pouring over the text, my notes, and coming up with a game plan for the next week's study. I spent hours reviewing material I had taught so many times before. As we drove to the biweekly meetings, Bev and I would discuss where the study was going that night, she would ask questions and give me hints as to how I might approach the topics of the evening. She was encouraging me to be free and say the things I saw in the text and from my study. Soon my attitude began to change.

One night as I was finishing the lesson and we were informally discussing its meaning, I saw something, something I had caught before, but not with the gravity as at that moment. The text was Rev. 5:1-9: I saw in the right hand of Him who sat on the throne a book sealed up with seven seals. And I saw a strong angel proclaiming with a loud voice, ***"Who is worthy to open the book and to break its seals?"*** And ***no one in heaven or on the earth or under the earth was able to open the book or to look into it.*** Then ***I began to weep*** greatly ***because no one was found worthy to open the book or to look into it;*** and one of the elders said to me, "Stop weeping; behold, ***the Lion*** that is from the tribe of Judah, the Root of David, ***has overcome so as to open the book and its seven seals."*** And ***I saw*** between the throne (with the four living creatures) and the elders a ***Lamb standing,*** as if slain, having seven horns and seven eyes, which are the seven Spirits of God, sent out into all the earth. And ***He came and took the*** **book** out of the right hand of Him who sat on the throne. When He had taken the book, the four living creatures and the twenty-four elders fell down before the Lamb, each one holding a harp and golden bowls full of incense, which are the prayers of the saints. And they sang a new song, saying, ***"Worthy are You to take the book and to break its seals.*** (author emphasis*)*.

The practical application I saw was so plain, so simple, but I had not fully appreciated or seen it in the light I did that night. I felt my broken, stone-cold heart twitch within me at the thought; "Jesus is the only one worthy to open the book and break its seals, and He took the book." My mind couldn't contain this wonderful truth, but my desperate spirit, now dead for over seven years, grabbed onto this first flicker of life. The translation? The book was my life, and no one, least of all me, was able or worthy to open the book of my life and look into it. Jesus alone could take the book of my life and break its seals and look into all that was planned for me. From deep within, I knew something had changed in that moment. Before, I had been a man at death's door: no pulse, no awareness, about to receive one more shock from a defibrillator and then pronounced "dead, we can do no more." But suddenly, I had the faintest pulse. It wasn't much to hang on to, but I set my only hope on it, and spent the next few months in intensive care, holding on to this lone fragile spark, tightly clinging to life.

I've heard it said, and believe its truth: Life begets life. It seemed almost immediately after the initial spark at that Thursday night Bible study, other sparks began to come, slowly at first, but steady and sure. As the study continued through the spring and into the summer, I felt more and more alive. That is not to say that I was out of the woods. My spiritual life still hung precariously close to the edge of an unimaginable abyss. I remained cynical of all things spiritual, and I struggled greatly to fan the small spark ignited on that night when I caught a faint glimpse of hope. But as the days went by, I could not deny that I was beginning to turn a corner and despair was giving way as the Father's unmistakable hand was gently leading me on.

Sometimes timing is the only difference between the dead ends in life and a door opening into a life only dreamed of. Such was the case for me as God began the process of resurrecting me. His timing was miraculous both in its schedule and its steady return in my troubled heart. One weekend late in the summer I had a bout with vertigo, even though I did not know that is what it was at the time. When I awoke one Saturday morning, I was dizzy and could barely stand. I fell back into bed as the room spun in circular motions. I tried to sit up and was overwhelmed and simply fell back again. I drifted to sleep and woke up feeling better, and thought that a shower would make me better still. I stepped into the shower, and as I turned to wash, it seemed like the outer walls of the bathroom collapsed, tile crashing through in a heap onto the ground outside. I woke lying on the bathroom floor, the shower curtain on top of me. I thought it was raining outside and it was splashing all around me. As

I regained my wits, I realized that the shower was running over my prone figure, and what a mess it made. I managed to get back to the bed and lay there. The phone rang, and I answered Bev's call. I was to meet her and a Cliffette at Daytona Beach that morning, but when she heard my garbled diction, she knew I was not well. I tried to tell her what I was feeling and she told me to just stay home. Her next call a few minutes later was to tell me to go to the hospital and she would meet me there. Our youngest son, John, was home and he went with me to Ocala, and I checked myself in. The emergency room personnel began running routine tests, getting my health history and so forth. By the time the test results came back, I was feeling much better and thought I'd go home that night. Bev and Cliffette arrived in the late afternoon. I was still in the emergency ward and the staff decided to keep me overnight for observation.

Those who know Bev know she is an avid reader. On her weekend getaway, she had read the new book, *The Shack,* by William P. Young. As I lay in my room that Saturday night, she told me, "You have to read this book. It's the best book I've ever read."

If I were to tell you about the best book I've ever read, you could rightfully take it with a grain of salt. I'm not much of a reader and rarely read anything for pleasure. I read for information and professional knowledge, and even that is a laborious chore to me. I'm not one who often recommends books to anyone. But when someone who has read the myriad of books Bev has, says, "This is the best book I've ever read," you sit up and take notice.

The days passed, and I still lay in the hospital. All symptoms of vertigo were gone but still the doctors wanted to run more tests. I decided to pick up this "best book Bev had ever read" and see what she was talking about. (If you haven't read this great book, you must. It is filled with nuggets of gold and you will learn about grace in a way that will do something for your soul. The book has induced a wide range of responses. There are those who think the story line *is* blasphemous, and there are others who think it sheds a magnificent light on our spiritual journey. Within those two extremes lies everything between, but for me, the book was more divine timing than theological treatise.) Early on as I read, the main character, Mack, is confronted with what he calls "a great sadness." It was that phrase that arrested my heart, and I would ponder it through the days, weeks, even the months that followed. Even now I return to that simple phrase with warmth, sadness, and wonder. Though I didn't relate to Mack's particular "great sadness," I knew my own. The dark corners of our lives often make us vulnerable to this kind of sadness and I was overwhelmed at mine. I cried uncontrollably as I read, alone in my room, in a hospital that would not release me to go home, reading a book whose grip on my soul captivated me, with a Father who would not let his wayward, lost son simply fade away. These deep sobs were my version of Rev. 5:4, "I began to weep greatly because no one was found worthy to open the book (*of my life*) or to look into it." This deep moaning that defies words was the first I had experienced in so long, and I felt it washing away the sadness and fear that had held me in its grasp and been my dark companion through the loneliest spiritual time in my life. My frigid heart began to break and melt, its stone coldness chipped and scraped into pieces and replaced by a new deep tenderness. The climactic moment of the book that finally broke me? The Father who knows everything there is to know about me, who knows all the reasons for my every dysfunction, who chooses to forgive even me, the most wretched of us all, and who calls me to Himself said, "I am especially fond of you."

A dam broke. I sobbed over my brokenness. I wept over the cold hardness of my heart and bemoaned the deadness of my soul. I wailed over the listlessness of my spirit and the "lostness", the "undoneness'" that was me. And at the same time, His presence, that had been my life's golden thread, returned, and my tears were turned to tears of uncontrollable joy and gratitude. I was rescued in that hospital room, and I was quickly becoming a new person. There had been a surgery in my very soul and I was spiritually resuscitated. I could breathe again, I could weep again, and most of all, I could feel Him again. The very next day I was discharged from the hospital, my thirty thousand dollar bill mysteriously paid in full, vertigo gone along with the stony heart that had held me its prisoner. I was alive again after eight long years. Though I had test after test in that five day stay, the hospital and all its doctors never discovered anything wrong with me. Just Vertigo!

Not long after my hospital revival, I visited with my lifelong friends, John and Terry Curington. John had been reading a book called, *He Loves Me,* by Wayne Jacobsen. As we sat outside by an open fire, John read from this book with tears on his face and a stirring in his heart. I was still enamored by, *The Shack,* and didn't fully appreciate John's tenderness at this book until I turned the first pages to read it. I immediately saw what had captivated John as he read.

I had long believed in the great love of God. Many of my favorite verses of scripture spoke of the reality that God loves, prince among these was John 3:16, "For God so loved the world that He gave His only begotten Son, that whosoever believes in Him should not perish, but have eternal life." In days gone by, I had preached more than one sermon that found its theme in the great love of God. But through the years of my cold death, I had been under such a barrage of thoughts about God's judgment and the feeling that He was so tired of me, that I had lost this most basic truth. In, *He Loves Me*, I saw myself on every page. The first heart-stopping chapter titled "Daisy-Pedal Christianity" hit me between the eyes. This chapter exactly captured my practical personal theology: it described a state of being in which we judge God's love for us by our circumstances or our actions, or lack of them. The Baptist version was "sins of commission and sins of omission." It seemed that they had me either way I went, and the cloud began to engulf me at an early age. If all went well in my life, it meant that He loved me. If things went badly, He was displeased with me and did not love me. In the book the author analogized this as the old, "He loves me, he loves me not" of childhood romance. Though I wasn't a child, my deep belief system had embraced this "Daisy-Pedal Christianity," if I was lucky enough, good enough, not bad enough, prayed enough, read the Bible enough, didn't "drink, smoke or chew" enough, then He would love me. But if I failed enough, if I blew it often enough, if I didn't do enough, then He loved me not.

As I read the book and pondered the deep questions at the end of each chapter, I gained a new practical spiritual theology. It's so simple I'm almost embarrassed to admit it. After all, I have seven years of higher education, three of those in theological studies. My "new spiritual theology?"—God loves me . . . period. He loved me before I had drawn my first breath and before I had done right or wrong. He didn't love me less when I failed. He didn't love me more because I succeeded. He just loved me despite my many failures or successes. He loved me though I sinned and lived below His desire for me. His love had been poured out on my life before the beginning and had been my constant through the variables that were my life and times. I could do nothing to earn it, stop it, dispel it, deserve it; it just was. I realized that I had lived most of my life trying to earn "points" with Him, like He had a heavenly chart, a scale that weighed the good things I did against the bad things I did. While I didn't believe this at a theological level, pragmatically speaking, it had been my theology all my life, this gray cloud, "If I do right, He loves me. If I do badly, He loves me not." And oh the cloud of guilt I carried for the missteps I took.

I felt myself being transformed as I read this small book. The truth that God loves me with a Father's love, no matter what, began to work in my heart, and I felt renewal as I turned each page. I openly wept as each chapter "nailed" me again. And with each nugget, life poured into my spiritual veins and with it, life restoring, soul freeing, heartwarming, life. As I felt my spirit becoming more alive, a new love for Him began to surface. And I again embraced a deep truth. Grace! Not a merit system; not a do-good-or-else; but a grace that loves the unlovely and wicked and that lavishly pours itself out on all who will dare to believe. That is more amazing than the sunset itself. As I pen these words, I feel it still. Grace so amazing, love so divine it covers all my yesterdays, all my todays, and every day yet to come. Such freedom this grace includes! I no longer had to "perform" or act like what I was not. I no longer had to pretend to be spiritual or have all the answers as I had thought in my young Bible school days. I certainly never had all the answers, but now I was free to not know and just receive His love and grace. What a wonderful work this truth has done in my being, an act in and of itself brought because of His great love and grace for me. He was redeeming the time, making the crooked way straight, and restoring my soul. I was feeling more alive with every breath I took. The life I had lived for those eight staggering years in the tomb was quickly falling away, and new life was pulsing through me again. It was more wonderful than I can put into words, and even so, God wasn't finished with me yet. I didn't know it then, and I don't fully understand it even now, but He had nothing short of full restoration on His mind. The long silence was over. I had gone through Death of a Vision and was beginning to feel a new, supernatural fulfillment of a vision that involved life, real, genuine life.

CHAPTER 17

He Restoreth My Soul

Long years ago, in the early days of my walk with the Lord, Bev and I had enjoyed the rich fellowship of Christian friends. We had spent large amounts of time together, some purposely spiritual, most simply relational. Bev also enjoyed the fellowship of other ladies as they joined together to make soap, to take the children to the park, to celebrate a one-year-olds birthday, to pick blackberries and can preserves, to create macramé plant holders and wall art, and a variety of other activities. Through those "non-spiritual" outings closeness was forged. A true sisterhood, a deep lasting bond, was made and nurtured that still stands strong today.

Likewise, I too had spent time with Christian men in those bygone days, camping in the wild or chatting over coffee at Wolfy's or IHOP or The Village Inn. We talked about politics, sports, and work frustrations, and we'd make jokes and laugh. We also talked about our young marriages and found that we were all pretty much the same, newly married or newly parents or struggling with money issues, scared we might fail or just trying to simply answer the old question, "What's it all about?" We learned to cry at our many common mistakes, and we learned to laugh at our many common mistakes, and we learned to hold each other and love each other through them all.

Additionally, Bev and I regularly and often found ourselves eating supper or playing cards or the game, Farkle, with these comfortable couples. We learned from each other as we tried to raise small children. We played racquetball late into the night or tried to catch a Frisbee while bouncing off the diving board into a swimming pool. We went to conferences and retreats together and prayed we wouldn't mess up as husbands and wives and parents, and we prayed that God would find pleasure in us and that we'd be found exactly where He wanted us to be. And all the time, real, authentic relationships were made. We were not just friends. What we had was more than friendships. We were family, Papa's family . . . AND then I went into "full-time vocational ministry," and everything changed.

The demands of a full-time job, regardless of vocation, can produce a juggling act with the many other components of one's life. Juggling a full-time job with all the other demands of life can be a tricky proposition indeed. Like a cake sliced in little pieces and given out at a party, often the slices quickly disappear, and someone gets left out. Many times the common casualty in this juggling act is authentic relationships. Sometimes you just run out of pieces of your time, sometimes someone gets left out, and sometimes, sometimes that someone is more important that you think.

My full-time job was church work, and I spent my days visiting the sick, the shut-ins, the hospitalized, new visitors to our church. I studied for Bible study groups and Sunday school classes and sermons. I counseled the distressed and the lovers wanting to get married. I attended ministerial meetings and denominational conferences. I worked church budgets and presided over church boards. I oversaw and was accountable for a variety of ministerial services, from cradle to grave. I performed weddings and dedicated babies; I officiated at funerals and provided grief counseling to those who remained. And, like many jobs, I was also responsible for a plethora of other things not found in any formal document. These ranged from getting the church van serviced to picking up the mail. These were my jobs.

Add to that, T-ball games, baseball and volleyball practices, gymnastics meets, spending time with aging parents and other important family get-togethers, obligatory "dates" with church leaders or parishioners where church work was the mainstay of conversation, and it's easy to see that the pieces of my cake were gone and there wasn't much time left for relationship building or nurture. We were always headed somewhere, it seemed, places to go, things to do, people to see, but not relationships to enjoy.

I was so full with the wonder of being "in ministry", the office door and parking space with my name, I hardly noticed the lacking relationships. I had quickly and excitedly begun busying myself with the ministry, but the excitement played out in short order, and before I knew it, I was hooked, reeled in, filleted, and being consumed at an alarming rate. Soon and very soon, it began to be all-consuming, and the juggling act began. I started sacrificing authentic relationships almost immediately and in less than sixteen years, I had let "ministry" take my life.

As I said in the last chapter, I am not an avid reader, so the fact that several books became part of my "awakening" heart is a minor miracle in itself. Of these I must mention just one volume more, *So You Don't Want to Go to Church Anymore* by Wayne Jacobsen and Dave Coleman. The title is perhaps most unfitting. The book speaks about relationships more than about organizations. It's only critical of the modern, organizational church in that we can "do" church at the expense of a personal relationship with Papa, and because this relationship is the spring from which all relationships flow, its presence or absence sets the tone for all other relationships. What struck me most is the fact that some of us can get so caught up in church functions, and church programs, we don't have time for the Father or relationships.

Looking back now, I can more clearly see the error of my thinking, but at the time, my demanding and misguided concept of ministry turned relationships, all relationships, into a means to an end—an agenda. There was almost no time available to be spent in easy conversations with old friends and new acquaintances. Rare was my time with brothers and sisters in Christ without my thoughts or conversations being led in the direction of church work. I was in the business of souls, or so I thought at the time, and every relationship, including friends and colleagues, even wife and children, was soon game to be hunted in order to feed that hungry hidden agenda.

I would eat breakfast periodically with old and dear friends, but these meals lacked the rich, meaningful conversations I had experienced before because I was always worried about some ministry that needed to be fixed or tweaked. I was always on the hunt for a new person who wanted to be a part of church work, and I harvested friendships instead of simply enjoying a relationship with them. Every gathering was an opportunity, not for real, genuine fellowship, but to tackle some church problem or fill some recent vacancy or get some new blood involved in the always insatiable ministry machine.

I was defensive when people posed their disappointment with church ministries saying they left no time or space for genuine relationships to emerge. I thought all that was needed was for them to get involved in some part of church work: teach that Sunday school class, take on the leadership of that church ministry, or get involved in filling that need. Then, as sure as sunshine follows a rain, deep relationships would come as the reward of "working for the Lord." Ironically, I was working constantly on church work, "working for the Lord," and I lived a lone, lonely existence. I was peddling a product that simply didn't work, and my own lack of deep relationships was evident proof of the fallacy I espoused. Even so, sometimes on those rare quiet moments of introspection and loneliness, sometimes even in the midst of the loud gongs and clanging cymbals and the relationship juggling of church work days, sometimes, somewhere deep inside me, I felt a whisper within that longed for the old friends of times gone by; no pretenses, no ulterior motives, no agendas, no programs, just the old friends I had left behind as I marched head long in "serving God" full time; friends with no other motive but true friendship and encouragement in our mutual walk of faith with the person of Jesus Christ.

Unfortunately, there was another relationship that was sacrificed on the altar of church busyness, the relationship with my own family. I had four kids who needed a father's attention, and I was rarely available at an emotional level for any of them. I had a wife who, while never demanding and always understanding and supportive, needed me. But I needed my cast of characters to perform as directed, to look a certain way, act a certain way, pretend if they must, but perform regardless. Don't get me wrong, I love my wife and my four wonderful children and always have. I never intended to make them puppets in a show. But this I certainly did. They were assistants in my business. I insisted that they simply must look and act the part and do nothing to upset anyone or embarrass me. Earlier in our marriage, Bev and I would talk and share dreams and ideas and desires late into the night. We'd speak of how the Father was leading and teaching us. Now we talked late into the night about how we would juggle this ministry, that denominational obligation, those nights away from home, who would take the kids to school that day, how would we get this child here and that child there at the same time. The whole juggling act left Bev empty, depressed, and drowning in a flood of performance theology, and I never even saw it. I never saw, let alone acknowledged the damage that the hurricane of my needs in ministry had caused in my own wife and children's lives, and I only see it now because Papa has opened my eyes and ears to see and hear, and that only in retrospect. But in the deep of my being, when the lights were off and all was quiet, oh how I wanted a change; how I wanted to return to those simpler times and cherished moments before I had been swept away with the ever rising tide.

Worse still, ministry as I was experiencing it relegated Bible study and prayer time to sermon preparation, Bible study teaching, and hospital praying. Gradually, my prayer times were public show more than heartfelt seeking after Him. I read the Bible for sermon material and prayed ministerial prayers to be heard by men, not the Father who loved me and could strengthen my wayward heart. I rarely sought His face or spent long moments touching His heart. My prayers were in times of crisis and pleas for help. I certainly never came to him to simply pour out my love on Him.

Nor were vacations times of spiritual renewal and refreshing. They didn't get me off the merry-go-round long enough to refocus on Him. The spiritual formation of my early adult life, times when I'd spend quiet mornings in a small unpretentious office in a corner of our house writing my prayers and spiritual observations for hours, the times I'd read the Bible, not for sermon fodder, but so I could be formed from within by Papa's thoughts, were no more. Gone too were the moments I'd set aside to meditate and contemplate on Him. No more personal retreats to a quiet place to walk and talk with my personal Savior and Lord, to hear His voice, still, small, powerful. Somehow the quest for doing things for Him had snuffed out the life that had been the motivation for the things in the first place. I had become far too busy to sit at His feet and learn of Him, and as a result I had no real, vital, personal relationship with the source of life, the Father of my soul. My pain at the loss of this most deep relationship was the most sharp of all.

These realities about my relationships while pursing ministry were poignantly articulated in the book, *So You Don't Want to go to Church Anymore*. I had to take personal stock as my heart was pierced by the truth I saw on the pages of this small book. I wasn't anti-church then, and I'm not now. I didn't mind going to church then, and I don't mind going now. I don't have an axe to grind with the ministry or the function of the spiritual gifts that enable it. I'm not on a crusade for or against church per se, but I now see more clearly that what I had been doing for the majority of my time in church work had made casualties of every relationship that mattered.

"But God," two of the most precious words ever placed together, set out to restore all the damage I had done, starting with the most important, my relationship with Him. He began in that small Thursday night Revelation Bible study. The longer that Bible study lasted, the sweeter it became. Starting with that first spark, He added such rich meaning and flooded my soul time and time again. He showed me new truths, and positioned me in the safest environment imaginable so He could nurture and love me. Of course He used brothers and sisters as His secret agents, but they knew, and I knew that they were just gloves into which He had slipped His healing hands. He brought me back from a depth of lostness I have no other way to describe other than calling it death, and let me feel again He who is beyond feelings. Sometimes, many times, I'd be so overwhelmed by a single simple nugget revealed to me; I'd ruminate and feed on it for weeks, all the while crying with deeper emotions than ever. A new gratitude also flooded my heart. I was spiritually breathing again. I had a spiritual pulse again. I was alive again, raised from the dead, and I was grateful and overwhelmed. The emotional contact with my Father was restored in full measure, in fuller measure that I could ever remember. So deep were my emotions being restored that I shared with close friends that it was as if I had had a stroke and all I seemed to do was cry. But this was so much more than mere tears. I was alive, and at every turn of the day I became more fully alive. Spending quiet moments with Him again added profound joy in my journey. He was all that was on my mind. He was the only topic I really wanted to discuss. His life in me, in us, was my most cherished center of conversational and meditational being. The hills of my heart were alive with the sounds of the sweet music of my salvation, wonderful, heartfelt songs of praise and thanksgiving to the Giver of life, to the giver of MY life, and the restorer of MY soul.

My relationship with Papa, my Father, Abba, had been restored. So wonderful this restoration, so rich this new found life, it was far more than worth the heart-ache that produced the death of all things in me. And the eight years in the clinched fist of death paled, faded, and was as nothing as I gazed into His face again. Many times, I'd sit in the backyard at my house at night, thinking of all He was doing in my heart and mind. I'd look up into the star-studded night, tears rolling down my cheeks, and whisper the words, "Thank you, Papa." This was no mindless mantra repeated to an impersonal deity. It was a powerful spontaneous flow of sincere gratitude to Him, not for food, shelter, cars, lands or anything else that might be pursued to add "meaning" to one's life. "Thank you, Papa" was the only thing that said all I had to say, and as I repeated it again and again I meant it more and more. Sometimes a song would be playing in the car whose theme was His amazing grace or his unfathomable mercy, and the tears would flow again as these great truths were more real to me than ever before. Through them, Papa reestablished me as his son again, prodigal—yes, wayward—yes, misdirected—yes, but son nonetheless. I felt Him there close, I heard His distinctive whisper, I smelled the unmistakable fragrance of His presence, and I handled His redeeming love with my own hands. Father to son, son to Father . . . I was restored!

One night in the late fall of 2008, as I sat outside, once again thanking Papa for all He had done and was still doing in my heart; for his restoration of my life and bringing me back from the dead, my thoughts turned to my children. They had been critically wounded in my ministerial years. Often uprooted from friends and the familiar, they had felt tossed here and yon as I made ministerial moves. They had been given the charge to be good little soldiers as they left friends behind and their daddy single-mindedly leapt across the country pursuing the ministerial dream with them in tow. They had endured a barrage of onslaughts from people who never took time to know them, and the whole experience had rightfully left a bad taste in their mouths.

We had never really sat down as a family or discussed those tough days when I was too busy or we were just not communicating, or when I was unavailable emotionally. I began to grieve over the lost years of their youth. Then, I had a "God idea." When I get an idea that is so simple to carry through yet carries such a potential weight of profundity that it cannot come from mere human thoughts, that's a "God idea." Mine was this: Set up with my children, each in turn, a time to share with them a brief history of my spiritual journey. I would share the "Readers' Digest" version of who I was spiritually, how I arrived at some of my most crucial decisions, and how it is that we landed where we were. The capstone of this time to share was to be my asking them to forgive me for not being a better dad, for often not being as engaged in their lives as I should have been, for my parental miscues, and things like that. Finally, I wanted to ask their forgiveness for my lack in drawing a picture in their hearts, a true picture of our heavenly Father, who was all about love and mercy and grace. I would ask them to forgive me, and place no ill will against the Father who loves them more than I do, and I would appeal to them to give Him a chance to show Himself to them, and allow Him to build a relationship with them.

Because Christmas time was so close, and because I've been told I'm hard to buy for, I suggested that for Christmas all I wanted was an evening alone with each one. We could go to a restaurant of their choosing for a meal, we could do anything they wanted, but I wanted a few uninterrupted hours to talk to them. Since we had never done anything like this, they were understandably suspicious of what I wanted to lay on them, and wondered what was up. I guess the mystery of the idea and what it meant and what its purpose was added an air of interest and probably a little anxiety to the meetings. My oldest son, Joseph, was first to schedule. I knew that he and his siblings were communicating about this meeting and as soon as we finished, he would call the others to fill in the blanks and help bring them up to speed.

Each meeting went well enough, as I shared the motives that had caused many of my choices in life. I shared some of the things contained in this book with each one. I asked for forgiveness just as I had planned. Each meeting was basically the same, though different in the personality mix of each. Joseph, ever the talkative and logical processor, said everything was fine. Christy, my only daughter, and known far and wide as the apple of her daddy's eye, cried as we shared these moments. Philip and John, more than any others, had been impacted by my church work. They had never known me as a present father. They were familiar with me interrupting vacation times to answer calls to the church. They knew me as the tired, often angry man who needed quiet so I could get a sermon together. They, along with Christy, were pushed to comply with dress codes and behavior codes so I would look like I had my house in order. They had felt the sting of ostracism or alienation produced by the fact that they were "the preacher's kids."

Philip and I simply built a fire in the fire pit at our house and talked into the night. He listened as I presented my case, and cried when I asked him to forgive me. Actually, in my thinking, something broke in him, and his cry turned to sobs as he asked me to forgive him too. I remember that as a special hour of time in my life. John and I met a few months later as he was being transferred to a new duty station in the Marines. On the trip, I shared my story, he listened, but it was clear to me that he was either in processing mode, or was not on any of the same pages as me. He forgave me nonetheless, and we enjoyed the hours of travel that remained.

For me, this simple idea was a new beginning with my children. I felt my heart shift again, and I was so grateful for each of them. In the longer term, I see a crack in their spiritual senses that I'm sure the Father will faithfully move through. I almost immediately felt a closeness to them I hadn't felt in a long time. They were gracious to me, telling me I was a good father, and I received that as a needed affirmation from them and Papa. I still long to fellowship with them on the deeper levels, about things that really matter, not just jobs and houses and lands. All my children seem to love being at home with Bev and I, and we have a lot of fun together. But the truth is this: they are in the Father's heart, on His mind, and in His plan. And I look on with eager eyes and open heart to see what He has in store for them. And I rejoice that the cold relationship of the past has been replaced with a deeper relationship built with them based not on a merit system of performance, but the solid rock of His mercy and grace and love.

Though we have always been close and enjoyed a rich relationship, even through the hectic years of juggling, Bev and I again talk late into the night, but now it's about what Papa has done and is doing in our lives and the renewal of our love. I discovered that she, too, had experienced a pain of soul produced by the lack of authentic relationship with our friends. I have asked her forgiveness time and again for my many slip-ups and failures, but she has remained my best confidant and friend and the most wonderful partner to walk this life with hand in hand. We hug and tell each other that we love each other, and we're experiencing a newness that only He can produce. And I shake my head in wonder and marvel again, and turn my face to heaven and whisper through broken voice, "Thank you, Papa!" I am restored with my family!

In my "dead years," as I call them, getting together with old friends was a social gathering only. In fact, I was always afraid that one of them would corner me somewhere, get all serious, and ask me where I really was with the Lord. I danced around that issue both figuratively and literally. As couples, we took ballroom dancing lessons, first by video, then in a studio. I was never destined to be Fred Astaire, but the lessons provided a safe place to not discuss my true place with the Lord, which at that time was no place at all. I tried to cover the darkness in my soul by humor. I tried to make people laugh and keep everything on a light-hearted level. I wasn't interested in the slightest hint of a spiritual conversation. That was in my "dead years!"

Now I was alive! New life was pulsing through me, a grateful heart beat in my chest, and a new and exciting fullness was coursing through my being. Now I longed for those conversations, I welcomed them, I sought them out. What Papa had done in my heart and life was all I wanted to talk about.

Back in the mid-seventies, a Christian music group called Love Song sang a song called "Welcome Back." It tells the story of a person who used to be a Christian but had sort of "dropped out" for a while, turned his back on the Lord, and for a season left the things he had believed in. The song then moves to the return of that one and the joy and love and acceptance afforded him when he came back. There was no "I told you so," no "have you learned your lesson," no condemnation. Just the arms-open acceptance and welcoming home to one who was battle-worn and bone-weary coming back into the full fellowship with his friends, and to Jesus.

This is how I was welcomed back and embraced by my longtime friends. So warm was their reception, it was as though I had never been gone. They listened to me relate where I'd been, what I had done, and simply rejoiced that I had returned. They told me that they knew I'd be alright, that I just needed some time. But I know better. They had stood vigil and prayed for me countless times during the years I meandered in lostness and death. And when it was over, no one rejoiced more than these true friends.

Of course we still go dancing together and love to fellowship around a table of food. We love to laugh and take small trips together. No one has to try to be anything other than who they are, but the new undercurrent for me is that I can join in the conversations of the great faithfulness of the Lord and His continual working in our lives. I see in their faces a contentment and profound joy in their walk that has sustained them through the years, and I can tell they are happy to have me back. As I write this page, the ready laughter and joyful conversations of these wonderful friends surround me as we camp on the beach together, and I think, "Thank you, Father!" I am restored to my friends.

It's always difficult, putting what one feels into words. What God has done for me is so much more than vocabularies and thesauruses can help explain. He didn't just restore my severed relationships with friends. He didn't just refresh my relationship with my kids. He didn't just bring me back to life again. These are more marvelous and wonderful than I can ever adequately articulate and He need not do anything more, but He has done even more. As I look around my life, I realize I've come full circle, and Papa has indeed restored my very soul.

CHAPTER 18

Your Turn

For well over a decade, I have taught English to seventh graders. My methodology has evolved over time, but mostly I have tried to explain concepts using PowerPoint presentations, question-and-answer techniques, group activities, and an endless array of examples and non-examples (a term that is only used in academia meaning: showing what not to do). I try to leave no stone unturned, to lay everything they need to know before them, and to give them ample opportunities to practice and question. I certainly never try to trick them or hide important information from them. Finally, at some point, after all the song and dance routines and all the hoopla and many "do-over's" of explanation and preparation, it is time to have the students do what I have been teaching and show that they have some degree of mastery of the skill I have been demonstrating. I always call this culminating evaluation, "Your turn."

I opened this book with these questions, "Why am I not that beggar without family, shelter, food? Why am I not the one with a sign in his hand and a pack upon his back? What did I do right that he did wrong? And, why is he not me?" Why indeed! Why am I not that beggar on the side of the road? Why am I not the lost one?

Of course the question could be expanded much further. Why am I not that one in a Siberian death camp or some other country where Christianity is illegal and punishable by death? Why am I not the one whose life is so impoverished that I would sell my children into slavery to help make ends meet? Why am I not the one scavenging to survive on a waste dump site in Calcutta? Why am I not the one born at a time of world wars and holocausts and great famines? Why was I spared the natural disasters that have plagued our world and swept away a countless host? Why was I not born addicted prenatally to crack cocaine, to a mother hopelessly addicted? Did I do something right that others did not? Was I standing at the right place at the right time when someone else wasn't? Is it that I am just a better class of person than others? Is it that I have tried to be more disciplined and principled than someone else? Is it just the luck of the draw that I was dealt the high cards in a cosmic poker game and someone else was dealt the low ones?

As concerns all the "why am I not's" I have no real answer. As for the questions about me possibly being inherently better than some else, this book gives a detailed elaboration to the emphatic answer, "No!" But as to why "me" I have one amazingly profound but simple answer: God's Amazing Grace! I say it again, here now, and will say it as my theme through all of time, "I am the passive beneficiary of a spiritual heritage that is mine simply because of the amazing grace of a sovereign God who chose to place me where I could not lose."

This story of my heritage, of my journey with Christ, of my struggles and missteps, of the aches of my life, of my quest to follow the Divine while living as a vessel of broken and flawed clay, of my failures and triumphs, and of my death and rebirth is not unique. God has chosen to shower each of us with amazing grace and mercy. He never waits for a blind follower to "get good enough" or somehow "qualify" before He sends His aide. He has already taken all the necessary steps to bring us, frail and dreadfully bound in human experiences, to Himself. None of us, especially me, could ever "qualify" for His smile of favor. So, He sends His grace first, and we are free to accept it if we choose. He initiates, and then, it's for us to embrace, or not. His mercy reaches to us; we must individually decide whether we will grasp it for ourselves.

This book is neither a theoretical credo nor a theological treatise born in the pages of books studied. Nor is it an attempt to reconcile the miscues and wanderings on my journey to faith, lost and found again. Nor is it intended to be a justification or atonement for my heart that has often strayed and stumbled and staggered at the Divine or His purposes for me. It is simply this: as honest a representation of His hand on my life as I can render. But if all you get out of this writing is knowledge of MY journey, you have missed the point entirely. If you only see Him carrying ME, continuing to pour out His mercy and grace on ME, still working on MY wayward heart, but fail to see yourself within the lines written here, this work will be nothing more than one man's spiritual journey, and if that's the case, it isn't worth the ink used to print the story. What does it matter that He chose me before I was born and called me to Himself? What difference does it make that He set before me a life lived in His hands and elected to call me His son? In the grand scheme of things, what difference does it make that He has been the orchestrator of a plan for me that spans the eternities past and future, a plan so wonderful and mysterious that I could never have envisioned and could never have realized it in my flesh in the smallest detail without His patient persistence and care. So, what then is the point?

Simply this: You have also been caught in the clinches of His grace, though you may have had no understanding that you were. He has set a path for you to travel, too. In the processes of your life, He has made Himself known to you in the steps and missteps you have taken. The twists and curves of your journey have been in His hands just as mine have, whether you have ever realized it. Like me, you have often been touched by the Divine, sometimes owning it completely; other times wishing He would leave you alone and let you be. And yet, you have known Him and have tasted His goodness through it all, and He still beckons you now. The deep cry within you to know He who is beyond being fully known, to follow Him, though you are unsure where He is leading you now or how He will get you there, that deep cry within you is clear evidence that He is orchestrating your life, too.

The common human story is that we all have tried to make our own way without Him. No matter, He still calls to your heart, His still, small voice still reaches to you now through the hurts and difficult decisions you have to make. He is undeterred in His pursuit of you, and His is a love that will not let you go. He has placed his hands on your life and will hold it to the end. Your mistakes and failures will never be more powerful than His grace, and in spite of all you have done or still do, maybe even because of them, He still holds you now.

It doesn't matter that you sometimes have misunderstood His leading even when you hungered for it more than anything else. He is big and strong enough to turn you toward Himself. This One is able to turn your heart like the water courses so that even when you misunderstand or misconstrue His leading, He brings you to the place that is uniquely yours. He isn't caught off guard when you fail, and He uses even failure to fulfill

His purpose in you. He redeems the wrong turns. He isn't disappointed when you stray. He isn't wearied by your many errors. He doesn't give up in frustration, and He isn't taken aback when you have wanted to give up, cash in your chips and quit. Even then, He stands right there, the unseen guide watching over and protecting you even from yourself.

The point is that my story is your story. The heritage of faith that has been given to me from "before the beginning," long before I was born, is your heritage too. It was initiated in the heart of God Himself before the first distant star, now long burned out and forgotten, was created. He has chosen you, and there is nothing you have ever done or will ever do that will ever change His mind about you. The scarlet thread that has run through our common heritage was no accident. You were His idea. And He will not let you go.

So, now you know the story and the story behind the story. The story is a living story, a story whose end has not yet been written. Have you caught the examples and non-examples and their significance? Do the explanations and anecdotes make it clear enough? Do you see the thread that has run through everything, even to this very moment right now? Will you chose His grace as your own? Will you embrace Him for yourself? Will you keep the scarlet thread of His grace for yourself and then pass its heritage to your posterity? Will you live your life in God's hands?

It's your turn!

Acknowledgements

How can I possibly thank and show full appreciation to those who have helped this dream become a reality? Many have expressed their encouragement as I have worked through the process and their spurring me on made such a difference in keeping me focused on the prize.

I am so grateful for the body of close friends who have read the divisions of the book as they unfolded. Of particular note is my small group of lifelong friends. This fellowship forms the real "church" in my life and has constantly proven their support at every turn. Some listened as I read a chapter and shared such enthusiastic applause. Others simply nodded their heads and prayed me through. These and my whole group have come together and were the friends "that sticks closer than a brother" as I lay in death and are to be credited in large measure to my being brought back to life.

I must name a few in particular. Lamar and Cliffette Holder are the ones who opened their heart and home for me to teach the book of Revelation where the spark of life ignited me again. They have read each chapter as they were completed and their joyful praise of my efforts has been a great source for keeping me writing. Bruce and Gail Ballard have also responded with such overwhelming support, dreaming big dreams for the far reaching possibilities that might be realized from this finished work. John and Terry Curington have cried with and prayed for me, believing in the great purpose that God placed in my heart from the beginning. Ed and Paula Plaster were always such constant encouragers and saw what I saw as I wrote. Finally, Tommy and Diane Wilson have been dear friends longer than I can remember and it was to them I first mentioned writing a book. Their response was magnanimous and motivated me to take the plunge and make the dream a reality.

My sister Ann Brack Lawrence has supported the writing of this story from the very beginning. She has worked to help authenticate and verify information and has contributed her editing expertise as well. She saved my life at the lake that April day and she has blessed my life more than I can say. My brother Gene, an amazing artist, supporter, and fellow sojourner encouraged me beyond words, and his handiwork created the cover for this book.

Emily Kuzneski Johnson, a dear colleague with whom I have worked for over eight years helped with the sizable task of editing my many miscues. Christi McKinney, Principal and dear friend also added richness to this work. Together, their professional understanding of writing and attention to detail has been invaluable.

Last, but most important, is my wife, Beverly. Her encouragement and constant support have really made this book possible. Most of the book takes place during our lives together. She has been a sounding board, a thinker, an editor, and my biggest cheerleader. She researched publishing alternatives and spent countless hours pulling together the multitude of strings to produce what you have read. She is the one person, more than any other that is responsible for this book. She caught my vision, held it close through the almost two year process, and never wavered. Her consistent, steady support has kept me focused and has helped make this the best book I can write. Without her aide and belief, this book would probably never have been written at all, certainly never completed as it is today. This is our story, not just mine.

Finally, I acknowledge the Great I Am, the God who is my Father, often called Papa in this work, who orchestrated my life depicted in this book. It was He who placed me in a long line of Christian heritage and saw to it that His crimson thread is continued through me. I owe all that I am to His grace and mercy and forgiveness. And it was His presence that moved me to write in the first place and to Him alone goes all the glory.